SEMANTICS

A NEW OUTLINE

F. R. PALMER

Professor of Linguistic Science
University of Reading

CAMBRIDGE UNIVERSITY PRESS

CAMBRIDGE

LONDON · NEW YORK · MELBOURNE

Published by the Syndics of the Cambridge University Press
The Pitt Building, Trumpington Street, Cambridge CB2 IRP
Bentley House, 200 Euston Road, London NWI 2DB
32 East 57th Street, New York, NY 10022, USA
296 Beaconsfield Parade, Middle Park, Melbourne 3206, Australia

© Cambridge University Press 1976

Library of Congress catalogue card number: 75-9089

hard covers ISBN: 0 521 20927 7
paperback ISBN: 0 521 09999 4

First published 1976

Composition by Linocomp Ltd., Marcham, Oxfordshire
Printed in Great Britain
at the University Printing House, Cambridge
(Euan Phillips, University Printer)

SEMANTICS

CONTENTS

PREFACE

This book is based upon a series of lectures on Semantics given at the Linguistic Institute in the State University of New York, Buffalo in 1971. It became clear that there was no elementary yet wide ranging work suitable as a very first introduction to the subject either for the student or the interested layman. The aim of this book is to provide such an introductory outline.

TYPOGRAPHICAL CONVENTIONS

SMALL CAPITALS

1. Technical terms when first introduced
2. Emphasis

Italics

1. Language material (to include technical terms when they themselves are the subject of discussion)
2. Foreign words
3. Titles of books

Quotation marks

1. Terms used in a semi-technical sense or terms whose validity is questioned
2. Meanings of words and sentences
3. Quotations and 'direct speech'

These conventions are used in the text, but not in displayed lists of words, diagrams or italicised headings

I

INTRODUCTION

SEMANTICS is the technical term used to refer to the study of meaning. Unfortunately, 'meaning' covers a variety of aspects of language, and there is no very general agreement either about what meaning is or about the way in which it should be described. I shall try to indicate both what topics are included in semantics and some of the ways in which they have been, or can be, handled. But because of the nature of the subject and the variety of views about it, I cannot hope to do more, in this little book, than to provide an introductory survey.

1.1 *The terms* semantics *and* meaning

The term *semantics* is a recent addition to the English language. (For a detailed account of its history see Read 1948.) Although there is one occurrence of *semantick* in the phrase *semantick philosophy* to mean 'divination' in the seventeenth century, *semantics* does not occur until it was introduced in a paper read to the American Philological Association in 1894 entitled 'Reflected meanings: a point in semantics'. The French term *sémantique* had been coined from the Greek in the previous year by M. Bréal. In both cases the term was not used simply to refer to meaning, but to its development – with what we shall later call 'historical semantics'. In 1900, however, there appeared Bréal's book *Semantics: studies in the science of meaning*; the French original had appeared three years earlier. This is a superb little book, now sadly neglected but well worth reading. It is one of the earliest books on linguistics as we understand it today, in that, first, it treated semantics as the 'science' of meaning, and secondly, that it was not primarily concerned with the historical change of meaning (see 1.4).

Yet the term *semantics* did not catch on for some time. One of the most famous books on semantics is *The meaning of meaning* by C. K. Ogden and I. A. Richards, first published in 1923. Yet *semantics* does not occur in the main body of the book itself. However, it appears in an appendix, which is itself a classic in the field, entitled *The problem of meaning in primitive languages*, written by the anthropologist, B. Malinowski.

Other terms besides *semantics* have been used. H. G. Wells in *The shape of things to come* speaks of the science of *significs*, but he says that it was lost sight of and not revived until the twenty-first century. Other names that have been used include *semasiology, semology, semiotics, sememics* and *semics*, though scholars have often used some of these terms to suit their own interests and orientation, and in both wider and narrower senses than our *semantics* will have here.

There is, unfortunately, a use of the terms *semantic* and *semantics* in popular language, especially in newspapers, that bears only a slight resemblance to our use. The terms are used to refer to the manipulation of language, mostly to mislead, by choosing the right word. Thus there were headlines in *The Guardian* in 1971: 'Semantic manoevres at the Pentagon' and 'Homelessness reduced to semantics'. The first of these headed an article in which it was suggested that the term *mobile manoevre* was being used to mean 'retreat', while in the second the point was rather that by using a very narrow definition of *homelessness* the authorities were able to suggest that the number of homeless was considerably reduced. There is a perfectly true story, too, of the strip-tease dancer who wrote to an eminent American linguist asking him to supply a word to replace *strip-tease* because of its 'wrong connotations'. 'I hope', she added 'that the science of semantics can help the verbally unprivileged members of my profession.' The eminent linguist, knowing his classical languages, suggested *ecdysiast*.

The term *meaning* is, of course, much more familiar to us all. But the dictionary will suggest a number of different meanings of *meaning*, or, more correctly, of the verb *mean*, and

Ogden and Richards were able to list no less than sixteen different meanings that have been favoured by 'reputable scholars'. It is no part of a book of this kind to investigate all these popular and scientific definitions of the term, nor to ask if all the meanings of *mean* and *meaning* have something in common. But a brief look at some of the common uses may be illuminating, for we can ask which, if any, of these comes close to the use of the terms that we need in semantics.

To begin with, we should not see a close link between the sense we require and the sense of 'intend' that we find in *I mean to be there tomorrow*. It is significant, perhaps, that we cannot, in this context, talk about 'my meaning', to refer to 'what I mean to do'. Much nearer to the sense we need is that of *Those clouds mean thunder* or *A red light means 'stop'*. For *mean* here (and *meaning* too) is used of signs, both natural and conventional, signs that indicate something that is happening or will happen, or something that has to be done. Such signs provide information or give instructions, and it is easy to assume that language consists of signs of a similar kind. When, however, we look at the use of the terms *mean* and *meaning* to refer to language we find that they seldom, if ever, suggest this notion of sign (though we shall soon see that many linguists have followed the analogy through).

The most relevant use of the terms for our purposes is found in such sentences as *What does 'calligraphy' mean? 'Calligraphy' is beautiful handwriting.* The reply to such questions is in terms of other words that the speaker thinks the hearer can understand. This is, of course, characteristic of dictionaries. They provide definitions by suggesting words or phrases which, we are given to understand, have the 'same' meaning, though what is same-ness is a problem that we shall not be able to escape (4.1). The extent to which meaning is dealt with in terms of the equivalence of terms is even more clearly brought out when we deal with foreign languages. For if we are asked what *chat* means in French we shall almost certainly reply 'cat'. It is interesting to notice that we would not ask what *cat* means in French, expecting the reply *chat*. In-

stead, we have to say *What is the French for 'cat'?* In stating
meaning, then, we are obliged to produce a term that is more
familiar than the one whose meaning is being questioned. We
translate from obscure terms, technical terms, or a foreign
language into words that can be easily understood. It is obvious,
however, that this will not get us very far in our study of meaning, for, though the principles of dictionary making may be
relevant to our enquiries, we are not solely, or chiefly, concerned with writing dictionaries.

A different use of *meaning* is found in such sentences as 'It
wasn't what he said, but what he meant.' Lewis Carroll made
play with the difference between saying and meaning in *Alice's
Adventures in Wonderland*:

> 'Then you should say what you mean', the March Hare
> went on.
> 'I do', Alice hastily replied; 'at least – at least I mean what
> I say – that's the same thing, you know'.
> 'Not the same thing a bit', said the Hatter.

This is a curious use for, if our words have a meaning, how can
we fail to say what we mean, or, rather, how can the words fail
to mean what they mean? The answer is, of course, that we
wish to suggest that the words do not mean what they might
most obviously be thought to mean, that there is some other
meaning besides the 'literal' meaning of the words. There are
a number of quite different ways of achieving this. We can
quite simply use such features as intonation or even perhaps
non-linguistic signs such as a wink to indicate that the words
must not be taken literally. In this respect there is one intonation tune in English that is particularly interesting – the fall-
rise, in which the intonation falls and rises on the 'accented'
word in a sentence. For this tune expresses reservations; it says
'but . . .'. For instance, with *She's very clever* it may well 'say'
(i.e. imply) that she is not very honest, or not very attractive,
while with *I think so* it would suggest that I do not really know
(whereas a different intonation would express confidence in
my belief). Similarly I can say, with sarcasm, *That's very*

clever to mean 'That's very stupid', and if I wink when I say 'That's mine', I probably intend to suggest that it is not. Secondly, much of what we say 'presupposes' a great deal. The classic example is *When did you stop beating your wife?* which presupposes that you beat her at one time without actually saying it. This, too, we shall have to discuss in detail later.

All in all, it seems that we shall not make much progress in the study of meaning by simply looking at common or even scholarly uses of the relevant terms. Rather we must attempt to see what meaning is, or should be, within the framework of an 'academic' or 'scientific' discipline. Semantics is a part of linguistics, the scientific study of language.

1.2 *Semantics and linguistics*

Let us now try to place semantics within linguistics and see what that implies. To begin with, we can assume that semantics is a component or level of linguistics of the same kind as phonetics or grammar. Moreover, nearly all linguists have, explicitly or implicitly, accepted a linguistic model in which semantics is at one 'end' and phonetics at the other, with grammar somewhere in the middle (though not necessarily that there are just these three levels). The plausibility of this is obvious enough. Language can be viewed as a communication system that relates something to be communicated with something that communicates, a message on the one hand with a set of signs or symbols on the other. The Swiss linguist, Ferdinand de Saussure, referred to these as the SIGNIFIER (*signifiant*) and the SIGNIFIED (*signifié*). (He, unfortunately, used the term SIGN to refer to the association of these two, but some of his more recent followers have, more reasonably, used it for the signifier alone.) Examples of communication systems, all of them no doubt much simpler than language, are numerous. For instance, traffic lights use a system of colours and colour combinations to instruct drivers to go or to stop (and also to warn that such instructions are about to be given). Similarly, animals make noises to communicate. The gibbons, for instance, have a set of calls to indicate the discovery of food, danger, friendly interest, desire for company, and they have one call that is intended merely to establish position and so prevent the band from spreading too far apart.

Although it is reasonable to see language as basically a communication system, we must not push the analogy with other systems too far, for several reasons. First, language does not always have a 'message' in any real sense, certainly not in the sense of a piece of information; part of its function is concerned with social relationships (see 2.4, 3.2), though this is also true of the animal communication systems too. Secondly, in language both the 'signs' and the 'messages' (the signifiers and the signified) are themselves enormously complex and the relationship between them is of even greater complexity. For this reason it has been convincingly argued that human language differs in kind rather than in degree from other 'languages'. Thirdly, in language it is extremely difficult, perhaps even impossible, to specify precisely what the message is. In other communication systems there is no problem because the message can be independently identified in terms of language or, rather, of A language such as English, e.g. *Red means 'stop'*. For language in general we have no such easy solution, for we cannot define meaning (the 'message') independently of language. We can only state one set of meanings in terms of another set, only describe language in terms of language.

I have suggested that linguistics is the 'scientific' study of language. One essential requirement is that it should be empirical. If semantics is part of linguistics it too must be no less scientific. Precisely what 'scientific' or 'empirical' means is a matter of some debate, but one essential requirement of a scientific study is that statements made within it must, in principle at least, be verifiable by observation. It is easy enough to apply this to phonetics, for we can observe what is happening – we can listen to a person speaking. We can, moreover, describe the operations of the vocal organs, or, with the aid of scientific instruments, can measure precisely the physical characteristics of the sounds that are emitted. But there is, unfortunately, no similar, simple, way of dealing with semantics.

Furthermore, if linguistics is scientific, it must be concerned not with specific instances, but with generalisations. This point was made, though in a rather different conceptual framework, by de Saussure in his distinction between LANGUAGE (*langue*) and SPEAKING (*parole*). This distinction has reappeared in the works of Noam Chomsky and his followers as COMPETENCE and PERFORMANCE. (Chomsky differs greatly from de Saussure on the nature of the linguistic system within language or competence, but the theoretical distinction is the same.) Both are concerned essentially, as are we, to exclude what is purely individual and accidental (speaking or performance), and to insist that the proper study of linguistics is language or competence. But for both de Saussure and Chomsky, language or competence is some kind of idealised system without any clear empirical basis, and I prefer to think rather in terms of generalisations.

The point is clear enough in phonetics. The phonetician is not primarily concerned with the particular sounds that are made at a particular time by a particular person. He may well study the pronunciation of e.g. *book*, but in order to do so he will listen to a number of individual utterances of this word and will make a generalised statement on the basis of these. Indeed, it is possible today, with the help of a computer, to produce an 'average' utterance, computed by the computer and produced by equipment that can reproduce human speech sounds. What happens at each time a person speaks is not usually of interest in itself; it is rather part of the evidence for the generalisations. The same must be true of semantics. We shall not normally be concerned with the meaning any individual wishes to place on his words. We may recall Lewis Carroll once again (*Through the Looking-Glass*):

> 'When I use a word', Humpty Dumpty said in a rather scornful tone, 'it means what I choose it to mean – neither more nor less'.

An individual's meaning is not part of the general study of semantics. Of course, it is interesting or important for some purposes to see how and why an individual diverges from the normal pattern. This is necessary in the study of literature – the poet may well not 'mean' what you and I would mean. It is obviously important too in psychiatric studies where the individual is apparently unable to use his language in the same way as others. But it is important to realise that neither the literary nor the psychiatric studies of the individual would be possible without the generalised 'normal' patterns to make comparisons with.

A useful distinction has been made between UTTERANCES and SENTENCES so that we can distinguish between the utterance 'There is a book on the table' and the sentence *There is a book on the table*. This may at first appear surprising and, unfortunately, the distinction is often lost because we talk of people 'uttering' or 'speaking' in 'sentences'. But the point is that an utterance is an event in time – it is produced by some one and at some particular time, while a sentence is an abstract entity that has no existence in time, but is part of the linguistic system of a language. The distinction is, obviously, related to that of language or competence and speaking or performance, the sentence belonging essentially to the former, and the utterance to the latter. It is important because when we talk about something that someone has said we normally describe it in terms that are appropriate to the sentence. In other words we use our linguistic knowledge (including what a sentence is) to talk about it. For instance, I referred to the utterance 'There is a book on the table', which may have been uttered by someone at some time. But in order to refer to it I have to write it down in words with all the conventions of spelling and punctuation. In so doing I identify it as an example of the sentence *There is a book on the table*. In order to talk about an utterance, that is to say, I have to treat it as an example of the generalised, more abstract, entity, the sentence. (The only way to avoid this completely would be to have the utterance on tape, for even writing it down in a phonetic script would probably assume some of the characteristics of the sentence.) In particular when I write it down I identify the words, but words are not a 'given' part of the utterance. They are not accessible by direct observation but are the result of some fairly sophisticated linguistic thinking (2.5). It follows from this that semanticists will not be (and cannot really ever be) concerned with the meaning of utterances, but only with the meaning of sentences, and it equally follows that we cannot study semantics without assuming a great deal about grammar and other aspects of the structure of language.

1.3 *The spoken language*

One important characteristic of the linguistic approach towards the study of language is that it is not concerned merely with the written language, but also (and usually with greater emphasis) with the spoken. There are at least four ways in which the spoken language is 'prior to', or more basic than, the written:

(i) The human race had speech long before it had writing and there are still many languages that have no written form.
(ii) The child learns to speak long before he learns to write.
(iii) Written language can, to a large extent, be converted into speech without loss. But the converse is not true; if we write down what is said we lose a great deal.
(iv) Speech plays a far greater role in our lives than writing. We spend far more time speaking than writing or reading.

The third point needs some explanation. There are a few features of the written form that are not easily (or not at all) represented in speech. For instance, the use of italics in this book to refer to examples would not be indicated if it were read aloud. Nor would the paragraphs, though that might not be a great loss. But the spoken language has far more striking characteristics that cannot be easily shown in the written form. In particular it has what are known as PROSODIC and PARA-LINGUISTIC features. The prosodic features include primarily what is usually handled under intonation and stress. We have already noted the use of a fall-rise intonation to suggest 'but . . .', and any speaker of English can easily become aware of the great use made of intonation for a whole variety of pur-

poses, largely of an attitudinal kind. The term STRESS is used
for several phenomena including the differences between e.g.
the verb *convict* and the noun *convict*, but for our purpose the
most interesting use is that which is sometimes referred to as
ACCENT (NOT in the sense of the different 'accents', i.e. dialect
features that people may have in different parts of a country),
in which the accent may fall on various words in a sentence.
Consider, for example, *Is Mary going to wear that hat?* The
accent may fall on any word (except, perhaps, *to*) with varying
implication – on *wear* it might suggest that she should eat it
instead! This kind of accent could, of course, be indicated in
the writing by italics or by underlining, but we seldom resort to
these devices and, in any case, the use of accent it not quite as
simple as this example would suggest. The semantics of intonation and stress is a major subject in its own right. But
meaning is also carried by paralinguistic features such as
rhythm, tempo, loudness (shouting and whispering are very
meaningful). In addition when we are talking we use many
non-linguistic signs (the term *paralinguistic* is sometimes used
for these too) – a smile or a wink may be as good an indication
that we do not really mean what we say as a 'sarcastic' intonation tune.

However, I shall not discuss the semantics of these features
in this book for three reasons – that the subject is a vast one,
that it is an extremely difficult one, since the meanings of the
prosodic and paralinguistic features are notoriously difficult to
define, and that (because of these two reasons) there is still little
agreement among scholars about the way to handle them. Yet
I confess that this is an unfortunate omission. Brief mention
of them will be made where they are directly relevant to some
semantically defined categories. Intonation cannot be left out
of the problem of speech acts (8.2), while stress is involved in
topic and comment (8.3). Many paralinguistic features too
should be involved in the question of speech acts, but as yet
no-one has attempted to correlate the two.

Even apart from the prosodic and paralinguistic features,
we have to recognise that the form of spoken language and the

purposes for which it is used are very different from those of the written. Concentration on the written language has misled grammarians – they have often failed to see that the spoken language is different from the written and have, misleadingly, attempted to describe the spoken language in terms appropriate to the written. It has been even more misleading for semanticists. For the written language is largely narration or the presentation of factual information or arguments. This has led to the assumption that meaning is largely concerned with information, with what philosophers have called 'propositions'. But the main function of language, especially the spoken language, is not to inform. It performs other and quite different functions as we shall see later (2.4).

1.4 *Historical semantics*

There will be virtually no discussion in this book (except in this section) of historical semantics, the study of the change of meaning in time. Yet a great deal of work that has been done on semantics has been of a historical kind, and it was noted earlier that the term *semantics* was first used to refer to the development and change of meaning.

Certainly the study of the change of meaning can be fascinating. We can start by attempting to classify the kinds of change that occur. The great American linguist, L. Bloomfield, noted a number of types, each given a traditional name. These, together with an example and the earlier meaning, were:

Narrowing	*meat*	'food'
Widening	*bird*	'nestling'
Metaphor	*bitter*	'biting'
Metonymy (nearness in space or time)		
	jaw	'cheek'
Synecdoche (whole/part relation)		
	town	'fence'
	stove	'heated room'
Hyperbole (stronger to weaker meaning)		
	astound	'strike with thunder'

Litotes (weaker to stronger meaning)

	kill	'torment'
Degeneration	*knave*	'boy'
Elevation	*knight*	'boy'

We shall also try to find reasons for the changes. Some are no more than fortuitous. The word *money* is related to Latin *moneo* 'warn' (cf. *admonish*), because money was made at Rome in the temple of the goddess Juno Moneta. The tanks of modern warfare are so called because of a security decision in the 1914–18 war to deceive the Germans into thinking that water-tanks were being despatched. Other changes arise from new needs. The word *car* was an obsolete poetic word for 'chariot', until the motor-car was invented. Most scientific words have acquired specialised meanings that have no close relationship to the non-scientific use; *mass* and *energy* in physics are not what they are to the layman. A cause of fast change is taboo – a word that is used for something unpleasant is replaced by another and that too is again replaced later. Thus English has had the terms *privy, W.C., lavatory, toilet, bathroom*, etc.

Historical change is properly an area of comparative and historical linguistics, or what is more commonly called COMPARATIVE PHILOLOGY, which attempts both to reconstruct the history of languages and, via their history, to relate languages apparently coming from a common source or 'ancestor'. One of the aims of the subject is to establish 'sound laws', to show for instance the correlation of *p* in Romance language with *f* in Germanic languages (this is an aspect of what is known as Grimm's Law). This can be illustrated in English where pairs of words come from Romance and Germanic, e.g. *father/paternal, feather/pen, fish/piscatorial*. But the establishment of sound laws depends on knowing that the words we compare are the 'same' in the sense that they can be supposed to have a common origin, and this can only be done on the basis of their meaning. This is obvious enough in the case of the examples above (remember that pens were originally quills). It is no surprise that we can relate *ewe* to Latin *ovis* 'sheep' and English *ovine*, or *acre* to Latin *ager* 'field' and agriculture. It may be more surprising (but only from the sound, not the meaning) that *cow* and *beef* are also related (though in a more complex way). Less likely in terms of meaning is the common origin of *guest* and *hostile*, until it is remembered that strangers might be treated either as friends or enemies. Generally the less obvious identifications of meaning are well supported by the evidence of sound laws. We find words that ought by the sound laws to be related, and then look for reasonable semantic relationships. Unhappily this is not possible with all groups of languages. In many parts of the world the language relationships are difficult to establish, largely because we have no ancient records. Thus speculation may take over. I have seen attempts to relate words from different African languages because of some phonetic similarity, but no sound laws, on the basis of the meanings 'day', 'sun', 'fire', and, similarly, 'sky', 'above', 'rain'. Unless the identification in terms of sound laws is convincing (and it is not), such identifications are not very persuasive.

Apart from the scientific study of the change of meaning, it is an obvious fact that people are interested in ETYMOLOGY, the discovery of earlier meanings of words (or, if we follow the etymology of *etymology*, the discovery of their 'true' meanings). Indeed dictionaries attempt to satisfy this interest by quoting at least the most recent origin of each word. Interest in etymology goes back for centuries. The first serious discussion is in Plato's *Cratylus*; many of the suggested etymologies there are preposterous, but a number of them are basically correct. Part of the difficulty for the layman is that words are often not what they seem. *Gooseberry* has nothing to do with geese, and *strawberry* is not directly connected with the use of straw to protect the fruit (though both *straw-* in *strawberry* and *straw* are from a common origin relating to strawberries strewing themselves and straw being strewn). But few would expect *hysterical* to be connected with the womb (in Greek), or for *lord* and *lady* to have anything to do with *loaf* (of bread).

Etymology for its own sake is of little importance, even if it has curiosity value, and there really should be no place for a smattering of it in dictionaries. The chief difficulty is that there can be no 'true' or 'original' meaning since human language stretches back too far. It is tempting, for instance, to say that *nice* REALLY means 'precise', as in *a nice distinction*. But a study of its history shows that it once meant *silly* (Latin *nescius* 'ignorant'), and earlier it must have been related to *ne* 'not' and *sc-* probably meaning 'cut' as in s*cissors* and *shears*. And before that? We cannot know. Clearly, then, there is no place for a serious discussion of etymology here.

As I said at the beginning of this section, there will be no further discussion of historical semantics. This may be surprising, and perhaps even disappointing, to the reader who has been led to believe by popular books and by the practice of most dictionaries to think of meaning in terms of change of meaning. But linguists have generally come to accept the distinction made explicit by de Saussure between DIACHRONIC and SYNCHRONIC linguistics, the first being concerned with language through time, the second with language as it is, or as it was at a particular time. Although there are some theoretical problems about drawing a clear line between these two types of study, in practice it can be drawn and a great deal of confusion can be avoided if we are clear whether a linguistic statement is a synchronic or diachronic one. For instance '*ought* is the past tense of *owe*', '*dice* is the plural of *die*' are confused statements. As synchronic facts about modern English they are untrue; they may be diachronically true – but in that case the verb should be 'was' not 'is'.

Linguists have in recent years concentrated on the synchronic study of language. It can, moreover, be argued that the synchronic study must logically precede the diachronic study, for we cannot study change in a language until we have first established what the language was like at the times during which it changed. So too in semantics we cannot deal with change of meaning until we know what meaning is. Unfortunately, because they have no clear theory of semantics, scholars interested in historical change have indulged in vague statements of the kind we considered earlier. This alone, I feel, is sufficient reason for concentrating, in a book of this size, on synchronic matters.

1.5 *Semantics in other disciplines*

Linguists are not the only scholars who have been interested in semantics. In particular the subject has been of interest to philosophers and psychologists. It is impossible to draw a clear line between what is a linguistic approach to the study of semantics and what is a philosophical or psychological approach, but we may point out some possible ways in which they may differ.

There is a considerable overlap between the philosophical and the linguistic approach to meaning, and a great deal of what philosophers have said, especially in the last thirty or forty years, is of interest to linguists. But we can identify some areas of divergence.

First, the linguist is not, or should not be, primarily interested in idealised systems of the kind found in some logical work. The logician's proposals have ranged from the comparatively simple syllogism of *All men are mortal. Socrates is a man. Therefore Socrates is mortal* to the highly involved 'logical syntax' of Rudolph Carnap. What they have in common is that they are not based upon observable language, but are essentially self-coherent and internally consistent models of an idealised kind similar to those of mathematics. In mathematics, of course, there is a distinction between 'pure' and 'applied', but there is little evidence of the possible application of logical systems to language and the linguist should be rightly suspicious of talk about 'the logical basis of language'. We shall in later sections discuss some logical or semi-logical approaches, but should always retain reservations about the degree to which such approaches can properly be made.

Secondly, there is a distinction to be made between science and the philosophy of science and here the approaches of the scientist and the philosopher will be very different. A rather striking example of this may be found in quantum mechanics. It can be stated that an electron is 'either at position A or at position B', yet it cannot be asked, even in principle, which of the two positions it occupies – whether it is at A and not B, or at B and not A. Similarly it can be said that an electron passed a barrier with two holes X and Y, and that it passed through X or Y, but it is not permissible to ask which hole it passed through, or to say that if it did not pass through X it must have passed through Y, and vice versa. This may seem to the 'ordinary man' to be an extraordinary state of affairs, but it is of no use for him to say to the scientist, 'How can that possibly be?' The scientist will merely reply by saying 'It is'. If pressed he can do no more than explain with the appropriate symbols and arguments why he regards his statements to be true. What the 'ordinary man' wants, of course, is not a scientific justification, but an explanation of the conceptual framework within which the scientific statements are made. 'What sense does it make to say such things?' is the kind of question he may ask. For an answer he must turn not to the scientist but to the philosopher of science who will attempt to explain the nature of scientific theory in general and of the particular 'model' of quantum mechanics.

It is worth noticing that there are two kinds of explanation here. First, the scientist explains the objects of his study by producing scientific rules for them. Secondly, the philosopher explains how the scientific explanations can themselves be understood.

The distinction between science and philosophy of science is less easy to make in linguistics because the 'facts' are so intangible, especially in the area of semantics. Indeed what we consider as facts will to a large extent depend on the framework, i.e. the model within which we describe them. But the distinction is still well worth keeping in mind, for it is all too easy to decide first upon the model and then state the facts within it, rather than attempting first to make empirical statements and then considering what kind of model is involved. Indeed a great deal of the arguments within the subject result from approaching the problems of semantics in this way. There will, naturally, be very little point of contact if one scholar starts with one model and another with another, instead of each, rather more humbly, attempting to see what first can be said and only subsequently building his model. In particular, for instance, there is something terribly wrong with a semantic model that simply excludes the use of language in context (see Chapter 5).

Psychologists have tackled semantics in several ways. One example is to be found in the works of Charles Morris, e.g. his book, *Signs, language and behavior*, published in 1946. In this book he is concerned with signs and what they denote or signify. Thus if a dog is trained to expect food when a buzzer goes, the food is 'denoted' by the buzzer (though if no food is provided it is not denoted but merely 'signified'). We shall return to discuss in detail this 'behaviourist' approach to meaning later (3.3). It is sufficient here to note that Morris compares the dog/food example with a man who prevents a driver from going along a road where there has been a landslide. Here the man's words are the sign, the landslide what is denoted, and 'the condition of being a landslide at that place' what is signified. But I find it very difficult to identify the use of the terms *sign, denote, signify* here with their use in the example of the dog and its food.

A very different, and less relevant, approach is found in a book entitled *The measurement of meaning* by C. E. Osgood, G. J. Suci and P. H. Tannenbaum. They attempt to 'measure' the meaning of words such as *father* in terms of semantic 'space', this space being defined in terms of a twenty-questions-like quiz: 'Is it happy or sad?', 'Is it hard or soft?', 'Is it slow or fast?' The results are plotted on a grid. But clearly this tells us little about meaning in general. It may say something about 'emotive' or 'connotational' meaning (see 2.4) such that *politician* will rate low and *statesman* high on the good/bad scale, but that is all.

There are, of course, many ways in which psychologists can observe people's reactions to various linguistic items – words, for example, in order to measure degrees of similarity, association, etc. The linguist, however, will feel that he is more interested in what actually happens in every day speech than in the artificial conditions of psychological experiments. For even if the subjects do react in certain ways, how is this to be related to their normal use of language?

A more promising approach might at first sight be found in an altogether different discipline, communication theory. In this theory we have several familiar concepts that are defined technically. The communication system carries INFORMATION and the system can be judged according to the efficiency with which it transmits the information. In particular an efficient system will have minimum REDUNDANCY (parts of the message that can be removed without removing any information) and minimum NOISE (anything at all that interferes with transmission). In language there is a great deal of redundancy and a lot of noise. A simple illustration of the redundancy in the written language is that if the bottom half of a line of print is covered the line can still be read. Noise may be just 'noise' in the usual sense, for that interferes with communication, but it can equally be loss of high frequencies on the telephone or radio, bad enunciation or bad handwriting or, in the example above, the covering of the bottom half of the line of print. In fact, there must be redundancy if a message can still be understood when there is noise. In semantics noise may consist of the discrepancies between the speaker's and the hearer's understanding – for this will interfere with the transmission of the information. But this theory will not help us a great deal with semantics, for information in the technical sense is not meaning. It is not the effectiveness of the transmission of information that concerns us in semantics, but precisely what that information is intended to be. The human speaker, unlike the communication system, does not merely transmit the message; he also creates it, and we cannot even begin to talk about information in this sense precisely because we cannot quantify or specify precisely what it is that is being 'transmitted'.

2

THE SCOPE OF SEMANTICS

In this chapter I shall attempt to clear the way for the consideration, in later chapters, of the various aspects of semantics, first, by discussing (and dismissing) two unsatisfactory views of semantics which, though prima facie plausible, provide no solution to semantic problems and, secondly, by attempting to set out some of the more important distinctions that have to be made.

2.1 *Naming*

In an earlier section it was suggested that language might be thought of as a communication system with on the one hand the signifier, on the other the signified. But a basic problem is to establish the nature and relationship of these two.

One of the oldest views, found in Plato's dialogue *Cratylus*, is that the signifier is a word in the language and the signified is the object in the world that it 'stands for', 'refers to' or 'denotes' (I shall use these terms without distinction – though some scholars have suggested that a useful distinction can be made). Words, that is to say, are 'names' or 'labels' for things.

This is, prima facie, an attractive view for it is surely true that the child learns many of his words precisely by a process of naming. He is often given names of objects by his parents and his first attempt at language will include saying 'Da da' when he sees his father or in producing his name for train, bus, cat, etc., on seeing the relevant objects in real life or in a book.

There are, however, many difficulties with this view. To begin with it seems to apply only to nouns; indeed traditional grammar often defines the noun, as distinct from the adjective, verb, preposition, etc., as 'the name of a person or thing'. It is difficult, if not impossible, to extend the theory of naming to include these other parts of speech. It is possible, no doubt, to label colours, as is done in colour charts, and thus it may be that the colour words (adjectives) can be regarded as names. But this is not at all plausible for most of the other adjectives. Since the beginning of this section I have used the adjectives *early, attractive, true, relevant, traditional, difficult* and *plausible.* How many of these could be used as a label to identify something that they denote? The point is even more obvious with verbs. It is virtually impossible to identify what is 'named' by a verb. Even if we take a verb like *run* and attempt to illustrate it with a boy running (either in a still or moving picture) there is no obvious way in which we can isolate the 'running' part of it. With a noun we can often draw a picture of the object that is denoted. But this is difficult, if not impossible, with verbs. For let us consider the verb *run* and an attempt to illustrate what it denotes with a picture of a boy running. There are two difficulties that arise (even if we have a moving picture). First, we are not presented separately with a boy and with 'running'. We need a fairly sophisticated method of separating the two. Secondly, even in so far as we can distinguish the boy and 'what he is doing', it is far more difficult to identify precisely what are the essential characteristics of what is denoted by the verb than what is denoted by the noun. For instance, does running involve only the movement of the feet or are the arms involved too? Does it necessarily involve a change of position? Is the speed relevant? Clearly there is not something that can easily be recognised and identified as 'running'. The problem is obviously even more difficult with *remember, like* or *see.* Similar considerations hold for prepositions (*up, under*) and conjunctions (*when, because*), while pronouns (*I, he*) raise even more severe problems, since they denote different things at different times.

Can we, however, retain the theory of naming, but apply it to nouns alone? An obvious problem, to begin with, is that some nouns e.g. *unicorn, goblin, fairy* relate to creatures that do not exist; they do not, therefore, denote objects in the world.

One way out of this difficulty is to distinguish two kinds of world, the real world and the world of fairy stories. But this is, of course, to admit that words are not just names of things, and it must involve some fairly sophisticated explanation of the way in which we can, by some kind of analogy, move from giving names to objects in the world to giving names to objects that do not exist. Such an explanation is possible, but such words are evidence of the fact that words are not simply names of the objects of our experience.

There are other nouns that, while not referring to imaginary items, do not refer to physical objects at all. Thus we cannot identify the objects to be named by *love, hate, inspiration, non-sense*. When the grammarians speak of nouns being names of things we can ask whether *love, hate*, etc., are things. If they are inclined to say 'Yes, but they are abstract things', it becomes clear that the only reason why they wish to call them things is that they have nouns corresponding to them. But then the whole definition is circular, since things are what are named by nouns (see 7.2).

Even where there are physical objects that are identifiable, it is by no means the case that the meaning is the same as its denotation (the object it 'stands for' or refers to). One of the best-known examples to illustrate this point is that of *the evening star* and *the morning star*. These can hardly be said to have the same meaning, yet they denote a single object, the planet Venus. Similarly, we may recall Gilbert and Sullivan's *The Mikado* where the titles *First-Lord of the Treasury, Lord Chief Justice, Commander-in-Chief, Lord High Admiral, Master of the Buck-Hounds* and many others all refer to Pooh-Bah.

Yet another difficulty is the fact that even if we restrict our attention to words that are linked with visible objects in the world around us, they often seem to denote a whole set of rather different objects. Chairs, for instance, come in all shapes and sizes, but precisely what is it that makes each one a chair rather than a settee or a stool? Often the dividing line between the items referred to by one word and those referred to by another

is vague and there may be overlap. For when is a hill a hill and
not a mountain? Or a stream a river? In the world of experience objects are not clearly grouped together ready, so to
speak, to be labelled with a single word. This is a problem that
has bothered philosophers from the time of Plato. There are
two extreme, but clearly unhelpful, explanations. One is the
'realist' view that all things called by the same name have some
common property – that there is some kind of reality that
establishes what is a chair, a hill, a house. The second, the
'nominalist' view, is that they have nothing in common but the
name. The second view is obviously false because we do not
use *chair* or *hill* for objects that are completely different – the
objects so named have something in common. But the first
view is no less invalid. For there are no clearly defined 'natural'
classes of objects in the world around us, simply waiting for a
label to be applied to them; part of the problem of semantics
is to establish what classes there are. Even if there are no
natural classes, it might be argued that there are 'universal'
classes, classes common to all languages. But this is not so. The
classification of objects in terms of the words used to denote
them differs from language to language. If, for instance, we
take the English words *stool, chair, arm-chair, couch, sofa,* we
shall not find precise equivalents in other languages. The
French word *fauteuil* might seem to be equivalent to English
arm-chair, but whereas the presence of arms is probably an
essential characteristic for *arm-chair*, this is not necessarily so
for *fauteuil*. Similar considerations hold for *chest of drawers,
side-board, cup-board, ward-robe, tall-boy,* etc. The colour
systems of languages appear to differ too (we shall discuss this
in more detail later), in spite of the apparently 'natural'
system of the rainbow. The words of a language often reflect
not so much the reality of the world, but the interests of the
people who speak it. This is clear enough if we look at cultures
different from our own. The anthropologist Malinowski noted
that the Trobriand Islanders had names for the things that were
useful to them in their daily life that did not correspond to
words in English (see 3.2). Another anthropologist, B. L.

Whorf, points out that the Eskimos have three words for snow depending on whether it was falling, lying on the ground or used for igloos, but only one word to refer to 'flier', be it an aeroplane, a pilot or an insect (see 3.4).

We can, unfortunately, be misled by scientific terminology for here we often find that there ARE natural classes. If we go to the zoo, we shall find that each creature has a particular name, and that no creature can be labelled in two different ways, nor is there any overlap between the classes. A gorilla is a gorilla, a lion a lion. The same is true, or very largely true, of the names of insects, plants and even of chemical substances. But these scientific classifications are not typical of everyday experience. Most of the things we see do not fall strictly into one class or another. Moreover, we should not be misled into thinking that we can and should tidy up our terminology by seeking the advice of the scientist. Of course, as literate and educated beings we will be influenced by scientific knowledge and may well refrain from calling a whale a fish or a bat a bird (though why could not fish simply mean 'a creature that swims in the water' and *bird* 'a vertebrate that flies'?). But we can go too far. Bloomfield argued that *salt* could be clearly defined as sodium chloride, or NaCl. He was wrong to do so. *Salt*, for ordinary language, is the substance that appears on our tables. It is no less salt if its chemical composition is not precisely that of the chemists' definition. *Salt* for most of us belongs with pepper and mustard, which do not lend themselves to any simple scientific specification – and neither should *salt* in its everyday use. Ordinary language differs from scientific language precisely in the fact that its terms are not clearly defined and its classes not rigorously established.

One possible way out of all our difficulties is to say that only SOME words actually denote objects – that children learn SOME of them as labels. The remainder are used in some way derived from the more basic use. This is in essence the proposal of Bertrand Russell who suggested that there are two kinds of word, 'object word' and 'dictionary word'. Object words are learnt ostensibly, i.e. by pointing at objects, while dictionary words have to be defined in terms of the object words. The object words thus have OSTENSIVE DEFINITIONS.

Yet much of what we have already said shows that this can be no solution. For in order to understand an ostensive definition we have to understand precisely what is being pointed at. If I point to a chair and say 'This is a chair', it is first of all necessary to realise that I am pointing to the whole object, not to one of its legs, or to the wood it is made of. That may be fairly easily established, but it is also necessary to know what are the characteristics of a chair if the definition is to be of any value. For someone who does not know already what a chair is may well assume from the ostensive definition that a stool or a settee is a chair. He might not even be sure whether the word *chair* applied equally to a table, since the ostensive definition does not even establish that we are pointing at a chair as something to be sat on, rather than as a piece of furniture. Pointing to an object itself involves the identification of the object, the specification of the qualities that make it a chair or a table. It requires a sophisticated understanding, perhaps even the understanding of the entire categorisation of the language concerned. As the philosopher, L. Wittgenstein, commented, 'I must already be the master of a language to understand an ostensive definition.'

To return to the child, it is clear enough that he does not simply learn the names of things. For if he did he would be unable to handle all the complexities that we have been discussing. Above all, learning a language is not learning just 'This is a . . .'; even less is it saying 'book' whenever he sees a book. We shall not solve problems of semantics by looking at a child learning language, for an understanding of what he does raises precisely the same problems as those of understanding what adults do in their normal speech.

So far in this section we have talked about the meaning of words. But we shall also have to discuss the meaning of sentences (Chapter 6). It is enough here to point out that a naming theory for sentences is no more satisfactory than one for words. We cannot directly relate the meaning of a sentence to things and events in the world. The strongest view which relates sentences to actual things and events, such that *There is a horse on the lawn* means that there is a horse on the lawn, is obviously untenable, since we can tell lies or make mistakes (there may be no horse on the lawn). A weaker view is to see meaning in terms of the conditions under which a sentence would be true – the meaning of *There is a horse on the lawn* being thus stated in terms of 'truth conditions' involving a certain kind of animal being at a particular time on a specially prepared area of grass. But this gets us nowhere. For the truth conditions can be most easily stated in the same words as the sentence – *There is a horse on the lawn* is true if there is a horse on the lawn (alternatively *There is a horse on the lawn* means 'There is a horse on the lawn'). The tautology is obvious – we are saying nothing at all. Putting the truth conditions into other words, moreover, e.g. paraphrasing in terms of 'an equine quadruped' does not help; it merely trades on some of the semantic relations within language (between *horse, equine, quadruped*) and totally fails, as does the naming theory of words, to specify meanings in terms of external things and events.

2.2 *Concepts*

The view we have just been criticising relates words and things directly. A more sophisticated and, at first sight, more plausible view is one that relates them through the mediation of concepts of the mind. This view in all its essentials has been held by some philosophers and linguists from ancient times right up to the present day. Two of the best-known versions are the 'sign' theory of de Saussure and the 'semiotic triangle' of Ogden and Richards.

According to de Saussure, as we have seen, the linguistic sign consists of a signifier and a signified; these are, however, more strictly a sound image and a concept, both linked by a psychological 'associative' bond. Both the noises we make, that is to say, and the objects of the world that we talk about are mirrored in some way by conceptual entities.

Ogden and Richards saw the relationship as a triangle.

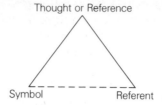

The 'symbol' is, of course, the linguistic element – the word, sentence, etc., and the 'referent' the object, etc., in the world of experience, while 'thought or reference' is concept. According to the theory there is no direct link between symbol and referent (between language and the world) – the link is via thought or reference, the concepts of our minds.

This theory avoids many of the problems of naming – the classifications, for instance, need not be natural or universal, but merely conceptual. But it also raises a completely new problem of its own. For what precisely is the 'associative bond' of de Saussure or the link between Ogden and Richards' symbol and concept?

The most naive answer to the question is to say that it is a psychological one, that when we think of a name we think of the concept and vice versa, i.e. that meaning consists of our ability (and indeed our practice) of associating one with the other, of remembering that *chair* refers to the concept 'chair'. This view is totally unsatisfactory. It is not clear what exactly is meant by 'thinking of' a concept. Some scholars have actually suggested that we have some kind of image of a chair when we talk about chairs. But this is certainly false. I can visualise a chair in 'my mind's eye', but I do not do so every time I utter the word *chair*. If this were a necessary part of talking, it would be impossible to give a lecture on linguistics. For precisely what would I visualise? The problem is, of course, that of names and things all over again. More reasonably, perhaps, what is meant is that I relate my utterance of the word *chair* to some more abstract concept. But that will not help either. For what is this abstract concept – what colour is this chair, what size or shape? In any case we ought not to be interested in what happens on each occasion, but with the more general question of the meaning of *chair*. As a phonetician, I should not be interested in the precise articulation of chair except as material for many more general statements of phonetics and phonology. Similarly, as a semanticist, I want to know about the general meaning of *chair*, not what I may or may not do every time I utter the word. As we said earlier we are not concerned with utterance meaning.

A more sophisticated version sees the link not as something we make every time we use a word, but as some kind of permanent association stored in the mind or in the brain. The difficulty with this view is that it really says nothing at all. For how can we, even in principle, establish what the concepts are? There is no obvious way in which we can look into our minds to recognise them, and still less a way in which we can look into the minds of others. In effect all this theory is doing is to set up, in some inaccessible place, entities that are BY DEFINITION mirror images of the words that they are supposed to explain. Wherever we have a word there will be a concept – and the concept will be the 'meaning of that word'. This is, obviously, a completely circular definition of meaning. It involves what is sometimes called a 'ghost-in-the-machine' argument. We wish to account for the working of a machine and present a total explanation in mechanical terms, but for some hypothetical person this is not enough – he cannot understand how this machine could work unless there is some kind of disembodied ghost or spirit inside it. Such an argument accounts for the phenomena by setting up an entity whose existence is justified solely as something that 'explains' the phenomena. Science has had many examples of this kind in its long history. Once scholars explained fire by positing the existence of the substance 'phlogiston'. Of course we can never disprove the existence of such entities. We can only point out that they explain nothing at all, and that, therefore, nothing is gained by arguing for them.

It is, perhaps, hardly necessary to point out that, as with

naming, the sentence is no more satisfactorily defined in terms of concepts than the word. Neither the naive or the more sophisticated version of the theory is at all helpful. Certainly when I say *There is a horse on the lawn* there is no reason to suggest that I actually 'think of' the concept, while a definition in terms of more abstract, timeless concepts is once again to say nothing at all but merely to interpret meaning by its mirror-image, postulated in an inaccessible place.

Sadly, there are many linguists today who accept in whole or in part a conceptual view of meaning. This has stemmed from a new 'mentalism' associated with N. Chomsky and his followers who have, in particular, insisted that intuition and introspection must play a large part in our investigation of language. It is a short and perhaps inevitable step to see meaning in terms of the mental entities called concepts. But this must be rejected for three reasons. First, the ghost-in-the-machine objection is overwhelming – nothing is said by moving meaning back one step to the brain or the mind. Secondly, even if there were concepts in the mind they are in principle inaccessible to anyone but the individual, and we are left therefore with totally subjective views, since I can never know what your 'meanings' are. (Of course, if we had the knowledge to investigate the brain scientifically and could account fully for language in the structure of brain cells, both of these objections might be, thereby, overcome, but we are centuries away from such knowledge.) Thirdly, the arguments about intuition and introspection are irrelevant. We CAN introspect – and ask ourselves questions about our language without actually waiting for empirical data, actual recordings or texts. But in so doing we do not learn more about our language or its structure; we merely produce for ourselves some more examples of our language. As J. R. Firth said, we go 'fishing in our own tank'. What we do NOT do by this process is establish the phonological or grammatical rules or structures; this comes from the investigation and comparison of a great deal of data (even if that data is all introspective). The same must be true of semantics, and it follows that we should not believe that there are concepts that can merely be discovered if we look in the right place. It is perhaps worth considering that if scientists had continued to rely on 'reason' (i.e. to look for answers to their problems within themselves and their own rational processes) rather than observation, we should still be searching for the philosopher's stone to turn lead into gold, rather than be on the edge of succeeding through nuclear physics.

Finally, in this section it is worth noting that to some extent DUALISM, the view of language described here and in the previous section that sees meaning as part of the signified/signifier relation, is encouraged by the term *meaning* itself and by the statement that words (and sentences) HAVE meaning. For if this is so it is obviously legitimate to ask what kind of entity meaning is, and to look for it either in the world or in people's minds. But to say that a word has meaning is not like saying that people have legs or that trees have leaves. We are easily misled by the verb *have* and the fact that *meaning* is a noun into looking for something that IS meaning.

In practice we all know what it is for a word to have meaning. Knowing the meaning of a word means that we can do a number of things – we can use it properly, we can explain it to others in terms of paraphrases or synonyms. But it does not follow from that that there is an entity that IS meaning or a whole group of entities that ARE the meaning of words. For a word to mean something is similar in some way to a notion that a signpost points somewhere; we can understand the meaning of a word just as we can read the signpost. But it does not make sense to ask what it is that words mean any more than to ask what it is that signposts point to. It is not sense, that is to say, to ask IN GENERAL what words mean or signposts point to. It is sense only to ask 'What does THIS word mean?', 'What does THIS signpost point to?'

The problem of semantics is not, then, nor can it be, the search for an elusive entity called 'meaning'. It is rather an attempt to understand how it is that words and sentences can 'mean' at all, or better perhaps, how they can be meaningful. If we are talking of 'having' meaning, it is rather like talking about 'having' length. Having length is being so many feet or inches long; length is not something over and above this. Similarly, meaning is not some entity that words or any other linguistic entities 'have', in any literal sense of 'having'.

Wittgenstein said, 'Don't look for the meaning of a word, look for its use.' This is not a very helpful remark since we are perhaps not much clearer about the 'use' of a word than we are about its meaning. But it has some value; we can investigate use, and we are less likely to think of use as something that words 'have' in any literal sense, and less likely to waste our time in an attempt to discover precisely what it is.

2.3 *Sense and reference*

I have already used the term REFERENCE in talking about the denotation of words in 2.1. It is also used in a useful, but wider sense, to contrast with SENSE, to distinguish between two very different, though related, aspects of meaning.

Reference deals with the relationship between the linguistic elements, words, sentences, etc., and the non-linguistic world of experience. Sense relates to the complex system of relationships that hold between the linguistic elements themselves (mostly the words); it is concerned only with intra-linguistic relations.

It might seem reasonable to argue that semantics is concerned only with the way we relate our language to our experience and so to say that reference is the essential element of semantics. Yet sense relationships have formed an important part of the study of language. For consider the words *ram* and *ewe*. These on the one hand refer to particular kinds of animals and derive their meaning in this way. But they also belong to a pattern in English that includes *cow/bull*, *sow/boar*, etc. Older grammars of English treated this as a part of grammar, because it was clearly related to sex, and sex was supposedly a matter of gender (since sex and gender are related in some degree in Latin). But there are other kinds of related words, e.g. *duck/duckling*, *pig/piglet* (involving adult and young), or between *father/son*, *uncle/nephew* (involving family relation-

ships), and these are not usually thought to be grammatical.
They are rather a part of the 'semantic structure' of English.
There are many other kinds of sense relations, too, e.g. those
exemplified by *narrow/wide, male/female, buy/sell*; these we
shall discuss in some detail later. The dictionary is usually
concerned with sense relations, with relating words to words,
though most dictionaries state such relations in a most un-
systematic way (Chapter 4). It could be argued, though, that
the ultimate aim of the dictionary is to supply its user with
referential meaning, and that it does so by relating a word whose
meaning is unknown to a word or words whose reference is
already understood.

We have, then, two kinds of semantics, one that deals with
semantic structure and the other that deals with meaning in
terms of our experience outside language. But the situation
should not surprise the linguist, since he has a similar situation at the other 'end' of his language model, where we had
tentatively placed phonetics (1.2). For linguists distinguish
between PHONETICS, which deals with speech sounds as such
and describes them in terms of their auditory or acoustic
characteristics or of the articulations of the speech organs, and
PHONOLOGY, which deals with the sound systems of languages
in terms of the internal relations between sounds. We might
well look for a similar distinction between 'semantics' and
'semology'. I shall not, however, use these terms because
reference and *sense* are in current usage. Nor would I push the
analogy too far. It is enough to see that there may be two kinds
of semantics, one that relates to non-linguistic entities, and one
that is intra-linguistic.

In recent years some linguists have attempted to limit
semantics, both in theory and in practice, to sense relations.
One example is to be found in a well-known article by
J. J. Katz and J. A. Fodor entitled, 'The structure of a semantic
theory'. (Katz and Fodor talk about 'sentences', whereas we
have been largely concerned with the meaning of words, but
their theory is based upon word meaning – and the question
whether the word or the sentence is the basic element of seman-

tics will be left until 6.1.) They state, 'A semantic theory describes and explains the interpretive ability of speakers: by accounting for their performance in determining the number of readings of a sentence; by detecting semantic anomalies; by deciding upon paraphrase relations between sentences; and by marking every other semantic property or relation that plays a role in this ability.' Stripped of its jargon this statement means that a semantic theory must account for ambiguity, anomaly and paraphrase (these will be explained and exemplified shortly).

The last sentence of the quotation is a most unfortunate one. It is a 'catch-all' qualification that effectively allows us to include in semantics all kinds of unspecified semantic properties or relations, but we may, presumably, assume that 'every other semantic property or relation' is of the same kind as the three that are given. Katz and Fodor give some examples of these, but a more complete and orderly list of semantic properties is to be found in an article by M. Bierwisch. He argues (following Katz and Fodor) that a semantic theory must explain such sentences as

(1)   *His typewriter has bad intentions.*
(2)   *My unmarried sister is married to a bachelor.*
(3)   *John was looking for the glasses.*
(4) (a) *The needle is too short.*
    (b) *The needle is not long enough.*
(5) (a) *Many of the students were unable to answer your question.*
    (b) *Only a few students grasped your question.*
(6) (a) *How long did Archibald remain in Monte Carlo?*
    (b) *Archibald remained in Monte Carlo for some time.*

(1) is an example of an anomalous sentence, (2) of a contradictory one and (3) of an ambiguous one (Katz and Fodor would say it has two readings); (4) illustrates paraphrase or synonymous sentences; in (5) one sentence follows from the other, while in (6) the first implies or presupposes the second.

Katz and Fodor quite specifically exclude from a semantic

theory any reference to the 'settings' of sentences. Semantics is not, or cannot be, concerned with the way words and sentences are used in relation to the world around us. Bierwisch, however, talks about (i) 'the interpretation of sentences' and (ii) 'how these interpretations are related to the things spoken about', but he gives no indication how we can proceed from the one to the other. Some linguists have even further restricted semantics and defined it in terms of truth-relations between sentences, i.e. those involving logical and analytic truth (see 6.4). Only some of the suggested sense relations will still belong to semantics. All meaning that does not belong to semantics is 'pragmatics'.

This is a really extraordinary state of affairs. What seemed at first to be the essential aspect of meaning, the relation between language and the world, is to be ignored or given second place. Moreover, only a tiny part of what is usually to be regarded as meaning can possibly be stated. For although dictionaries are concerned with defining one word in terms of others and so with sense, only a minute part of dictionary definition could be handled in terms of the sense relations we have listed (but see Chapter 4). Sadly, one is tempted to conclude that when scholars have concentrated on sense to the exclusion of reference (in its widest sense), they have done so because it is easy to describe. It has structure and can be accurately and precisely determined. But this reminds one of the drunk who lost his key at his front door but was found looking for it under the street-lamp ten yards away 'because it's lighter here'.

There are some further difficulties. It is not always possible to distinguish clearly between sense and reference for the simple reason that the categories of our language correspond, to some degree at least, to real-world distinctions. Whether language determines the shape of the world or vice versa is probably a 'chicken and egg' problem, though it will be discussed in 3.4. The fact that we have *ram/ewe, bull/cow* may be part of the semantic structure of English, but it also clearly relates to the fact that there are male and female sheep and cattle. But we have to remember (1) that not all languages will make the same distinctions, (2) that there is considerable indeterminacy in the categorisation of the real world – as we saw in our discussion of names, some things (e.g. the mammals) fall into fairly natural classes, others do not. It is because of this that we can (a) distinguish sense and reference, yet (b) must allow that there is no absolute line between them, between what is in the world and what is in language.

Some scholars have been very concerned by the fact that if we deal with meaning in terms of the world, then semantics must include the sum total of human knowledge and for this reason have restricted their attention to sense. This argument is discussed in detail in 3.1, where it is argued that the problem of the sum total human knowledge is no less a problem for sense. Moreover, there are some terms of language that are not reducible to other terms, but interpretable ONLY in terms of the events around us. Most important are the DEICTICS (what philosophers have called 'indexical expressions'), the pronouns, *I, you,* etc., the demonstratives *this* and *that* and time markers such as *now* and *tomorrow* (7.4). For these cannot be paraphrased by any other forms that do not themselves indicate the real world, the present time or the relevant speakers and hearers. A theory of meaning in terms solely of sense, of intra-linguistic relations, cannot even in principle handle these terms. Only a theory that accepts the relation of language to the world can do so. There is, of course, the added bonus that such a theory can handle other kinds of meaning too (next section).

2.4 *Kinds of meaning*

Implicit in the view of semantics as a study of sense relations (and even more obviously as a study of truth conditions) is the assumption that it is concerned with factual information or with 'propositions' that can be either true or false.

No doubt this is one of the aspects of meaning that has to be considered, what has variously been called 'cognitive', 'ideational', 'denotational' or 'propositional' meaning. But it is by no means the only kind of meaning and it is not even clear that it is the most important. Certainly we should not wish to say that the prime or only function of language is to provide information, to inform hearers or readers of 'facts' that they do not already know (though some linguists and philosophers have believed this). A great deal of our meaning is not 'ideational' at all, but is 'inter-personal' or 'social', relating ourselves to others. There are a number of ways (not all distinct) in which we can see that language is not simply a matter of providing factual information.

First, we do not merely make statements; we also ask questions and give orders. Indeed, the grammars of most, if not all, languages reflect these distinctions by having question forms and imperatives (though the grammatical function does not always correspond with the distinction between stating, asking and ordering – what is grammatically a statement can be semantically an order, e.g. *You're coming tomorrow*). It seems easy enough to handle questions in terms of information, since they are obviously requests for information; they can thus, in part, have an ideational meaning. But it is much less clear how we can handle orders in a similar way; they are concerned with getting action, not information.

Secondly, there are a variety of what today are called 'speech acts'. We persuade, we warn, we insinuate; we use language, that is to say, to influence other people in many different ways. This is the first aspect of language that a child learns – he discovers that by using his cries he can attract attention and then that the appropriate speech will manipulate adults into giving him food, playing with him, etc. This aspect of language has recently come to interest linguists, but its relation to ideational meaning is not at all clear yet (see 8.2).

Thirdly, much of what we say is not a statement of fact but an evaluation. Some semanticists have made a great play with the emotive difference between *politician* and *statesman*, *hide* and *conceal*, *liberty* and *freedom*, each implying approval or disapproval. The function of such words in language is, of course, to influence attitudes. There are far more subtle ways than saying something is good or bad or even of choosing the 'good' or a 'bad' word. In politics particular words are often chosen simply for the effect they are likely to have. *Fascist* no longer refers to a member of the fascist parties, it is simply used to condemn and insult opponents. Words may have different emotive meanings in different societies. On the whole *liberal* is a 'good' word in Great Britain – even used by Winston Churchill of himself when he was politically a Conservative, but it is a 'bad' word in South Africa and in some political circles in the United States. This emotive or evaluative function of language is by no means confined to pairs of words such as these. Indeed there are not many words that the dictionary has to mark with such labels as 'derog'. But there are many other words for which part of the meaning is 'good' or 'bad', such as *palace, hovel, hero, villain,* and, of course the words *good* and *bad* themselves do not indicate 'fact', but are indications of evaluation. There will be some further discussion of this in the section on synonyms (4.1).

Fourthly, language is often deeply concerned with a variety of social relations. We can be rude or polite, and the decision to be one or the other may depend upon the social relationship with the person to whom we are speaking. Thus we may ask for silence with *Shut up, Be quiet, Would you please be quiet?, Would you keep your voice down a little please?* The choice depends on whether we wish to be rude or not – and this relates to the status of the person addressed. Some parts of language are wholly social and carry no information (even if we include giving orders, etc., within information) at all. Examples are *Good morning, How are you?,* and all the Englishman's remarks about the weather. In most societies replies and questions are often about the family, but no real information is being sought – the speaker does not want to know about the health of the wife of the man he is talking to, but is simply making social contact. Even a great deal of 'small talk' at parties is really of the same kind. It is not intended to transmit information, but is simply part of the social activity. As W. S. Gilbert said (*Patience*):

> The meaning doesn't matter
> If it's only idle chatter
> Of a transcendental kind.

Fifthly, as we have already noted, we need not 'mean what we say'. We can by the appropriate use of intonation be sarcastic, so that *That's very clever* means, 'That's not very clever'. We can also with the appropriate intonation imply what is not said. Thus *I don't like coffee* with a fall-rise intonation may well imply *I like tea* and *She's very clever* may suggest *She's rather ugly*. The moral of this is that semantics cannot fully succeed without an investigation of the prosodic and paralinguistic features of language (see 1.3 and 8.2).

Sixthly, there is the kind of meaning found in the notorious *When did you stop beating your wife?* For this presupposes that you once beat her, though it nowhere states that you did. Similarly it has been argued that *The King of France is bald* presupposes that there is a King of France and that presupposing his existence does not assert it. Presupposition is thus distinct from assertion. The subject of presupposition will be dealt with in 8.4.

There may, of course, be other kinds of meaning. Notice also that if someone says *There's a house over there*, I may ask, *What does that mean?*, i.e. *What am I to conclude from that?* Although this is close to the first sense of meaning that we discussed in 1.1, it will be clear now that this kind of 'meaning' is surely outside semantics. It is concerned with the way we may use information, but in particular cases, and so is a matter essentially for utterance-meaning.

2.5 *The word as a semantic unit*

It is normally assumed that dictionaries are concerned with words and that therefore the word is, in some sense at least, one of the basic units of semantics. Yet there are some difficulties.

First, not all words seem to have the same kind of meaning. A very familiar distinction is that made by the English grammarian, Henry Sweet, between 'full' words and 'form' words.

Examples of full words are *tree, sing, blue, gently* and of form
words *it, the, of, and.* Only full words seem to have meaning
of the kind we have been interested in so far. The form words
seem to belong to grammar rather than to semantics; more
strictly they belong to grammar rather than to lexicon (see 7.1).
They can still be said to have meaning, but meaning of a
grammatical kind. Yet this is not so much the meaning of the
word itself but rather its meaning in relation to the other words,
and perhaps to the whole sentence. We should not, for that
reason, wish to look for the meaning of such words in isolation,
but only within the sentence. (Dictionaries often attempt to
define them, but with little success.)

Secondly, it is not at all clear that the word is a clearly defined unit, except as a conventional one resulting from the rules
for writing that we all have learnt at school. Words as we know
them are the written items between which we have learnt to put
spaces. But we may well question whether this is necessarily
an indication of a well-defined linguistic element. In Arabic
the definite article is written as part of the word; in English
it is not. There are no clear criteria for deciding which of these
is the more appropriate. Or let us compare *greenhouse* with
White House (in *The White House*). Apart from our conventions of spacing are there good reasons for saying that the
former is one word, the latter two?

Bloomfield offered a solution by suggesting that the word is
the 'minimum free form', the smallest form that may occur in
isolation. But this all depends on what is meant by 'in isolation'. For we shall not normally say *the, is, by* in isolation. We
might, of course, produce these 'words' in reply to a question
such as *What is the second word here?* or *Did you say 'a' or
'the'?* But this just begs the question. We learn to utter in
isolation just those items that we have learnt to recognise as
words. Bloomfield went on to identify an element smaller than
the word, a unit of meaning – the MORPHEME: examples are
-berry in *blackberry* or *-y* in *Johnny*. Later linguists were more
interested in the status of such words as *loved* where they could
identify the morphemes *love-* and *-d.* Here the two elements

seem clearly to have the distinct meanings of 'adore' and 'past'. But problems soon arose especially with words such as *took*, which appears to be both 'take' and 'past', yet cannot easily be divided. The purely grammatical status of such words is not our concern, but we must recognise that there are two independent 'bits' of meaning. The best way to handle this is not in terms of morphemes (i.e. parts of words), but rather by redefining the term *word* in a different, though not unfamiliar way. We have been using this term in the sense that *love* and *loved* are different words. But we could also say that they are forms of the same word – the verb 'to love' (which, oddly enough, we identify by using two words, *to* and *love*). A technical term for the word in this second sense is LEXEME. It is lexemes that usually provide dictionary headings. There will not be two entries for *love* and *loved*, but one only (and this may even include the noun *love* as well as the verb, though we may not wish to extend the term *lexeme* in a similar way). If we proceed on these lines we can talk about the meaning of words (i.e. lexemes), and independently of the meaning of grammatical elements such as plural or past tense. Instead of treating *loved* as the two morphemes *love* and *d*, we shall analyse it in terms of the lexeme *love* and the grammatical category of tense. This solution leaves us with the word (defined as the lexeme) as the unit for our dictionary. But we are still left with the meaning of the grammatical element. Sometimes it may seem to be fairly simple and independent, e.g. plural which means 'more than one' (but see 7.2). But often this is not so. Case in Latin largely marks relations within sentences – the subject, the object, etc. Gender, too, in Latin is only superficially concerned with the physical feature of sex, and its main function is to indicate grammatical relations – that a certain adjective modifies a certain noun, etc. (see 7.3). The status of these elements is thus often not very different from that of the form words we discussed earlier.

Thirdly, there is a problem with what have been called TRANSPARENT and OPAQUE words (Ullmann, 1962). Transparent words are those whose meaning can be determined from the meaning of their parts, opaque words those for which this is not possible. Thus *chopper* and *doorman* are transparent, but *axe* and *porter* are opaque. Comparison with other languages, German in particular, is interesting. In English *thimble, glove* and *linguistics* are opaque (the same is true of the equivalent French words, too); in German the corresponding words are all transparent – *Fingerhut* ('finger-hat'), *Handschuh* ('hand-shoe'), *Sprachwissenschaft* ('language-science'). This suggests not only that one word may be seen as consisting of several bits of meaning, but also that the number of 'bits' is arbitrary. (Do we look for elements of meaning in *thimble* because of the German word?) There are problems of detail too. If we decide that chopper is to be interpreted in terms of *chop* and *-er* (indicating the instrument), what do we say of *hammer*? Is this transparent? The *-er* shows that it is an instrument, but what is 'hamming'? There is, then, no precise way of determining the semantic elements within a word.

Fourthly, there are many words in English that are called PHONAESTHETIC, in which one part, often the initial cluster of consonants, gives an indication of meaning of a rather special kind. Thus many words beginning with *sl-* are 'slippery' in some way – *slide, slip, slither, slush, sluice, sludge*, etc., or else they are merely pejorative – *slattern, slut, slang, sly, sloppy, slovenly*, etc. The *sk-* words refer to surfaces or superficiality – *skate, skimp, skid, skim, skin*, etc. The reader may consider also the meaning of words beginning with *sn-, str-, sw-, tw-*, etc. An amusing set is that which ends in *-ump*; almost all refer to some kind of roundish mass – *plump, chump, rump, hump, stump,* and even perhaps *dump* and *mumps*. But we cannot generalise too far. Not every word with these phonological characteristics will have the meaning suggested, and, moreover, we cannot separate this part and state the meaning of the remainder, e.g. the meaning of *-ide* in *slide* or *-ate* in *skate*.

Fifthly, semantic division seems to 'override' word division. Consider, for example, *heavy smoker* and *good singer*. Semantically these are not *heavy + smoker* (a smoker who is heavy) and *good + singer* (a singer who is good). The meaning rather is one who smokes heavily or sings well. We can divide, if we insist, but the first division has to be between *heavy smok-* and *-er, good sing-* and *-er*, if we want to retain the parallelism between the form and the meaning. Further amusing examples that have been suggested are *artificial florist* and *criminal lawyer*.

Sixthly, although we have *ram/ewe, stallion/mare*, we have no similar pairs for *giraffe* or *elephant*. We have to say *male giraffe, female giraffe*, or if we know the correct term *elephant bull and elephant cow*. Such considerations, together with the fact that we have the words *cow* and *calf*, may lead us to define *bull* as *male adult bovine animal* and to see this as an indication of four distinct elements of meaning in the same word.

Finally we have the problem of idioms. By an IDIOM is meant a sequence of words whose meaning cannot be predicted from the meanings of the words themselves. Familiar examples are *kick the bucket, fly off the handle, spill the beans, red herring*. The point is clear if we contrast *kick the table, fly off the roof, spill the coffee, red fish*. Semantically, idioms are single units. But they are not single grammatical units like words, for there is no past tense **kick the bucketed*. There will be a more detailed discussion of idioms in 5.3.

All these considerations may lead us to abandon the idea that the word is a natural unit for semantics, however useful it may be for the dictionary maker. C. E. Bazell commented, 'To seek a semantic unit within the boundaries of the word simply because these boundaries are clearer than others is like looking for a lost ball on the lawn simply because the thicket provides poor ground for such a search.'

Yet we must be careful. We must not conclude from all this that we can simply ignore the words of the language and instead look for independent 'meanings', for semantic entities, that is to say, that are totally unrelated to words. (On such a view it is only when we have done the semantic analysis that we will attempt to relate our semantic units to those of the grammar, including words.) That this is quite unacceptable is shown by the discussion in this book. For throughout we have been establishing meaning by comparison of linguistic forms, almost always involving words. Idioms are notable only because they consist of several words but function like one, while in discussing morphemes, transparent words, phonaesthetics and all the rest we were nearly always comparing words with words. We shall sometimes have semantic units larger than the word and often semantic units smaller than it (or at least allow that one word may have more than one 'bit' of meaning). But we shall never get away from these linguistic forms to some 'disembodied' meanings. For consider *bull* again. There is nothing here to indicate size, weight, colour, speed, fitness, etc., yet these could all be regarded as relevant to its meaning. It is, rather, only those features that are brought out by contrast with *cow* and *calf* that are relevant to semantics, i.e. only those that depend upon word contrasts.

Chapter 4 will be called *Lexical structure*. This is to emphasise the point I have just been making. The alternative title *Semantic structure* might suggest that we can look for meanings and relations between them divorced from the forms of language.

3

THE NON-LINGUISTIC CONTEXT

In the last chapter a distinction was drawn between reference, which deals with the relations between language and the non-linguistic world of experience, and sense, which deals with relations within language. Linguists and philosophers have, on the whole, been more concerned with sense relations. Sense relations appear, superficially at least, to be easier to handle than reference is; a great deal of this book will, in consequence, be concerned with sense. Yet most people would think that meaning was primarily (or even wholly) concerned with the relation between language and the world in which we use it. For this reason I shall begin this chapter by dealing with reference. But I shall not use the term 'reference' for two reasons, first, that it is ambiguous, and that it has the narrower sense of the denotation of words (and we are concerned here with the wider sense only) and, secondly, that the term CONTEXT or, to distinguish it from the linguistic context, CONTEXT OF SITUATION is more familiar within linguistic discussion.

3.1 *The exclusion of context*
We have already noted that there are linguists who, explicitly or implicitly, exclude context from the study of semantics. The real reason, no doubt, for this exclusion is that there are extremely great theoretical and practical difficulties in handling context satisfactorily. But reasons other than these are often given, and these we will now consider.

First, it is argued that the meaning of a sentence, or the fact that it is ambiguous or anomalous, can be known in isolation from any context, and that as speakers of a language we must know the meaning of a sentence before we can use it in any given context; meaning is thus shown to be independent of context and linguists can, and must, study it without reference to context. This argument, however, begs the question. For in what sense could it be argued that we know the meaning of a sentence independently of the context? Presumably, only in the sense that we can provide another sentence of similar meaning, a paraphrase of it. But it in no way follows that if we can identify two sentences as having the same meaning, we have, thereby, identified some abstract entity called 'meaning'. This is another version of the dualist fallacy that we discussed at the end of 2.2. Instead, it might well be argued that knowing that two sentences are similar in meaning is knowing that they can be used in similar contexts. In that case, to set up a set of abstract relationships between sentences without even considering what it is that they refer to, is rather like describing all the equivalences in a measuring system, e.g. that there are twelve inches in a foot, three feet in a yard, 1760 yards in a mile, without even indicating how long an inch, a foot, a yard or a mile actually is. Stating meaning equivalence is not stating meaning, and there is no proof that knowing the meaning of a sentence does not entail knowing the context in which it is used.

A second and, at first sight, rather more plausible argument is that the world of experience must of necessity include the sum of human knowledge. If this is so, and if semantics is defined in terms of reference, the scope of semantics will be infinite. This is a problem of which Bloomfield was aware, and it made him despair of any satisfactory treatment of semantics. But the problem is one that is raised for any kind of comprehensive theory of semantics. It is no less acute for a theory based on sense relations than one based on reference, for it is impossible even in that theory to draw a clear line between the meaning of a word or sentence and all the possibly relevant information about it. We can evade the problem by confining our attention to 'tight' logical relationships of the kind seen in *unmarried/bachelor* or *short/long*, but this will provide a very narrow semantic theory that can hardly be said to deal properly with meaning. For consider the sense relations involved in Bierwisch's *My typewriter has bad intentions* (which is anomalous) and *John was looking for the glasses* (which is ambiguous). To recognise the anomaly and the ambiguity we need to have the relevant information about typewriters and kinds of glasses.

To make this point clear let us consider, in a little detail, part of the argument of Katz and Fodor. It will be remembered that part of the aim of semantics according to them was to 'account for the number of readings of a sentence'. An example was *The bill is large*. This is clearly ambiguous – it has two 'readings' resulting from the two meanings of *bill*. The sentence can, however, be 'disambiguated', i.e. one or other of its two readings can be established if we extend it with . . . *but need not be paid*. This extension is, of course, possible only with one of the meanings of *bill*. Now Katz and Fodor accept that the ambiguity of this sentence and its disambiguation by this method are proper subjects for semantics. Yet the discussion of them is immediately followed by the argument against a 'complete theory of settings' (i.e. context) that such a theory would have to represent all the knowledge that speakers have about the world. This point is illustrated by the fact that ANY kind of non-linguistic information may be used in the understanding of a sentence. One set of examples they use to show this is *Shall we take junior back to the zoo? Shall we take the bus back to the zoo? Shall we take the lion back to the zoo?* To understand these, it is suggested, we have to know all about boys, buses and lions, and that such information cannot be included in a semantic theory. Yet a moment's reflection will show that the position is no different than with *bill*. For on the one hand it seems reasonable to say that we need the information that there are two kinds of bill. On the other hand we can extend these other sentences to show the meaning differences with . . . *to see the other animals?*, . . . *or walk?*, . . . *or put it in our own cage?* Now I think it is obvious that we can always invent extensions to sentences to deal with any kind of 'meaning' relating to any kind of information that may be relevant. If this is so, and if the use of such extensions is a valid method of establishing sense relations, it follows that ANY kind of information can be the basis of a sense relation and that sense, no less than reference, ultimately involves the whole of human knowledge.

Let us take another example, Bierwisch's *John was looking for the glasses.* This is ambiguous because it might refer to spectacles or to drinking glasses. But why should there be just two meanings? What if a scientist has yet a third type? Does the sentence now have three meanings? If it does, it does so because of our knowledge of the world. Similarly, how many meanings has *I am looking for the bible*? The answer depends on whether you know that one of the cow's stomachs is called *the bible*! Similarly, let us take Bierwisch's anomalous example *My typewriter has bad intentions*, and replace *typewriter* by *dog, snake* and *microbe.* Whether the resulting sentence is judged to be anomalous can be determined only by what we know about the intelligence of dogs, snakes and microbes. The anomaly depends, that is to say, on knowledge of the world.

Katz and Fodor admit that a limited theory of selection by 'socio-physical settings' is possible, but say that this would blur the distinction between the speaker's knowledge of his language and his knowledge of the world. But the distinction is blurred (or is, in principle, impossible to make) anyway.

There is, then, no such thing in semantics as linguistic ability that is unrelated to knowledge of the world. These are essentially one and the same thing. That does not mean, of course, that we cannot in some way limit our area of study, but it is a mistake to think that we can limit it to what is 'purely' linguistic.

3.2 *Context of situation*

The term *context of situation* is associated with two scholars, first an anthropologist who has already been mentioned, B. Malinowski, and later a linguist, J. R. Firth. Both were concerned with stating meaning in terms of the context in which language is used, but in rather different ways.

Malinowski's interest in language derived from his work in the Trobriand Islands in the South Pacific. He was particularly concerned with his failure to produce any satisfactory translations for the texts he had recorded. For instance, he recorded a boast by a canoeist which he translated, 'We-run front-wood ourselves . . . we-turn we-see companion-ours he-runs rear-wood.' This, Malinowski argued, made sense only if the utterance was seen in the context in which it was used where it would become clear that, for instance, 'wood' referred to the paddle of the canoe. Living languages must not be treated like dead ones, torn from their context of situation, but seen as used by people for hunting, cultivating, looking for fish, etc. Language as used in books is not at all the norm; it represents a far-fetched derivative function of language, for language was not originally a 'mirror of reflected thought'. Language is, he maintained, a 'mode of action' not a 'countersign of thought'.

Malinowski's arguments were primarily based on his observation of the way in which the language of the people he was studying fitted into their everyday activities, and was thus an inseparable part of them. But he noted also that there is, even in our own more sophisticated society, a special significance of expressions such as *How do you do? Ah, here you are*, which are used to establish a common sentiment. We noted a number of examples of this – talk about the weather or the family in 2.4. This aspect of language he called 'phatic communion', where the words do not convey meaning but have a purely social function.

He noted, too, that the child, right from the stage of babbling, uses words as 'active forces' with which to manipulate the world around him. For the primitive man, similarly, words are 'important utensils'. Indeed for him, Malinowski argued, there is much in common between words and magic, for both give him power.

Malinowski's remarks about language as a mode of action are useful in reminding us that language is not simply a matter of stating information. But there are two reasons why we cannot wholly accept his arguments. First, he believed that the 'mode of action' aspect of language was most clearly seen in the 'basic' needs of man as illustrated in the languages of the child or of primitive man. He assumed that the language he was considering was more primitive than our own and thus more closely associated with the practical needs of the primitive society. To a very large degree, therefore, he assumed that the difficulties of translation were due to the differences in the nature of the languages and that the need to invoke context of situation was more important when dealing with primitive languages. But he was mistaken. For although there may be 'primitive' people, who lack the knowledge and skill of civilised people, there is no sense in which a language can be regarded as primitive. Of course many languages may not have the vocabulary of modern industrial society, but this is a reflection of the interests of the society, not of the primitive nature of the language. In purely linguistic terms it appears to be a fact that no one language can be judged more primitive than another – though Malinowski is by no means the only scholar to make this false assumption. The difficulties of translation that Malinowski noted result only from the DIFFERENCES between the languages, not the fact that one is more primitive. Secondly, Malinowski's views do not provide the basis of any workable semantic theory. He does not even discuss the ways in which context can be handled in a systematic way, to provide a statement of meaning. Moreover, it is quite clear that even with his Trobriand Islanders much of their linguistic activity is not easily related to context. For instance, he discusses narrative, the telling of stories; but here, surely, the context is the same at all times – the story teller and his audience, whatever the story. If context is to be taken as an indication of meaning, all stories will have the same meaning. Malinowski's solution was to invoke 'secondary context', the context within the narrative; but that has no immediately observable status and can no more be objectively defined than concepts or thoughts that he was so eager to banish from discussion.

J. R. Firth, the first Professor of General Linguistics in Great Britain, acknowledged his debt to Malinowski, but felt that Malinowski's context of situation was not satisfactory for the more accurate and precise linguistic approach to the problem. For Malinowski's context of situation was 'a bit of the social process which can be considered apart' or 'an ordered series of events *in rebus*' (i.e. an ACTUAL observable set of events). Firth preferred to see context of situation as part of the linguist's apparatus in the same way as are the grammatical categories that he uses. It was best used as 'a suitable schematic construct' to apply to language events and he, therefore, suggested the following categories:

A.   The relevant features of the participants: persons, personalities
    (i)   The verbal action of the participants.
    (ii) The non-verbal action of the participants.
B.   The relevant objects.
C.   The effects of the verbal action.

In this way contexts of situation can be grouped and classified – and this is, of course, essential if it is to be part of the linguistic analysis of a language.

As an example of his use of context of situation Firth considered a 'typical' Cockney event with the sentence:

'Ahng gunna gi' wun fer Ber'.'

'I'm going to get one for Bert.'

'What', he asks, 'is the minimum number of participants? Three? Four? Where might it happen? In a pub? Where is Bert? Outside? Or playing darts? What are the relevant objects? What is the effect of the sentence? "Obvious!" you say.'

It is important to stress that Firth saw context of situation as one part of the linguist's apparatus or rather as one of the techniques of description, grammar being another such technique on a different level, but of the same abstract nature. For linguistics was for him a sort of hierarchy of such techniques all of which made statements of meaning. Here he used the analogy of the spectrum in which light is dispersed into its various wavelengths; linguistics similarly would 'disperse' meaning in a 'spectrum of specialized statements'. Thus, for Firth all kinds of linguistic description, the phonology, the grammar, etc., as well as the context of situation, were statements of meaning. Describing meaning in terms of context of situation is, then, just one of the ways in which a linguist handles a language, and not in principle very different from the other ways in which he carries out his task.

Firth's views have often been criticised or even rejected outright, but the criticisms have usually failed to understand precisely what Firth was trying to say. It will be worth while, therefore, to consider some of them since this may make Firth's standpoint clearer.

First, it has often been said that he was guilty of equivocation in his use of the word 'meaning'. For while context of situation may well deal with meaning in the usual sense, i.e. the 'semantic' sense, quite clearly the other levels, grammar, etc., are not concerned with meaning in the same sense. In claiming, therefore, that all the levels are statements of meaning and that context of situation was thus just one of a set of similar levels, Firth was, consciously or unconsciously, using 'meaning' in two different senses, one legitimate, the other his own idiosyncratic usage.

This criticism is not entirely fair for three reasons. First, it is valid only if we accept that there IS an area of linguistic investigation which deals with the relation of language and the world outside that is quite distinct from the investigation of the internal characteristics of language. But, as we have already seen, many linguists have confined semantics to sense relations; for them at least, the study of meaning does not differ greatly in kind from grammar, since both would seem to be intralinguistic. I do not accept this point of view – I merely point out that Firth is by no means alone in seeing the study of meaning in the narrow semantic sense as not different in principle from the study of grammar. Secondly, we have already seen in the discussion of sense and reference (2.3), that it is almost certainly impossible, in principle, to decide what is 'in the world' and what is 'in language'. If this is so, Firth is surely to be

praised rather than criticised for refusing to draw a clear distinction within his levels of description between the one that
deals with language and the world and those that are wholly
within language. Thirdly, Firth did not produce any total,
'monolithic', linguistic model which could, in theory at least,
totally describe a language. He did not, in fact, believe that
such a model was possible even in principle (though nearly
all linguists have assumed that such a model is not merely
possible, but essential). The linguist for Firth merely makes partial statements of meaning, saying what he can about language
where he can, cutting into it at different places like cutting a
cake. There is no need on such a view to distinguish between
statements that are about meaning and those that are not.

A second criticism of Firth's view is that it has very limited
value since it will not get us very far. Context of situation may
be all right for the Cockney example or for the drill sergeant's
Stand at — ease, but not for the vast majority of the sentences
that we encounter. But this does not prove that Firth was
wrong. If we cannot get very far with context of situation this
is perhaps no more than a reflection of the difficulty of saying
anything about semantics, and it is surely better to say a little
than to say nothing at all. It must be remembered too that
Firth believed we could never capture the whole of meaning.
The proper conclusion, perhaps, should be that we need far
more sophisticated techniques for context of situation than
have yet been developed.

It is easy enough to be scornful, as some scholars have been,
of contextual theories and to dismiss them as totally unwork-
able. But it is difficult to see how we can dismiss them without
denying the obvious fact that the meaning of words and sentences relate to the world of our experience. One virtue of
Firth's approach was that he set out to make only PARTIAL statements of meaning. It may be that this is all we can ever hope to
achieve.

3.3 *Behaviourism*
Malinowski and Firth believed that the description of a

language could not be complete without some reference to the context of situation in which the language operated. A more extreme view sees the meaning of the linguistic elements as TOTALLY accounted for in terms of the situation in which it is used; the situation, moreover, is wholly definable in empirical or physical terms.

This is BEHAVIOURISM, associated first in linguistics with Bloomfield. Bloomfield's starting point was not so much his observation of language events as his belief in the 'scientific' nature of his subject and he maintained that the only useful generalisations about language are 'inductive' generalisations. He defined the meaning of a linguistic form as 'the situation in which the speaker utters it and the response it calls forth in the hearer'. This is going much further than either Malinowski or Firth. They made statements of meaning in terms of the situation. Bloomfield is, essentially, defining meaning AS the situation.

Bloomfield illustrated his views with a now famous account of Jack and Jill. Jill is hungry, sees an apple and with the use of language gets Jack to fetch it for her. If she had been alone (or if she had not been human) she would have first received a STIMULUS (S) which would have produced a REACTION (R) (the term RESPONSE is more usual) – she would have made a move to get the apple. This can be diagrammed

Since, however, Jack was with her, the stimulus produced not the reaction R, but a linguistic reaction, that of speaking to Jack, which we may symbolise r. The sound waves resulting from this in turn create a stimulus for Jack, a linguistic stimulus (s), which results in his non-linguistic reaction R of getting the apple. We now have a more complicated picture

Meaning, according to Bloomfield, consists in the relation between speech (which is shown by r . . . s and the practical events (S) and (R) that precede and follow it.

One important point for the theory is that the stimulus and the reaction are physical events. For Jill it is a matter of light waves striking her eyes, of her muscles contracting and of fluids being secreted in her stomach. Jack's action is no less physical.

Bloomfield was at great pains to contrast his 'mechanistic' theory with the 'mentalistic' theories that posit non-physical processes such as thoughts, concepts, images, feelings, etc. He did not deny that we have such images, feelings, etc., but explained them as popular terms for bodily movements, events that the speaker alone is aware of (as in *I'm hungry*), private experiences (obscure internal stimuli), or soundless movements of the vocal organs. Moreover, he included in the situation all the relationships that hold between Jack and Jill. Jill might not have acted in the same way if she had been bashful, and Jack might not have fetched the apple if he had been ill-disposed towards her. This means that the speech and the practical events depend upon 'predisposing factors' which consist of 'the entire life history of the speaker and hearer'.

Now it may well be that ultimately all activity is, in principle, explainable in terms of physical entities and events, the chemistry, electro-magnetism, etc., involved in the cells of the human brain. But this is, in the light of present human knowledge, no more than an act of faith, a simple belief in the physical nature of all human activity. For linguistics, however, the theory has no value. The facts, especially those concerning predisposing factors, are totally unknowable and no more open to observation than the thought, images, etc., of the mentalists that Bloomfield despised. In the present state of our knowledge talking about predisposing factors involves the same circularity of argument as talking about concepts (2.2).

Bloomfield had a curious and rather misplaced faith in science and scientific description. He forecast (quite incorrectly as it turned out) that all the problems of phonology would be solved in a few decades in the phonetics laboratory. More pertinently, he suggested that we can define the meaning of a speech form accurately 'when this meaning has to do with some matter of which we possess scientific knowledge' and gave as an example the 'ordinary meaning of salt' as 'sodium chloride (NaCl)' (see 2.1). Apart from the fact that it is not clear how this meaning is related to the model of meaning illustrated by Jack and Jill (possibly a matter of ostensive definition?), it is surely clear that Bloomfield is factually wrong. There is no reason at all to argue that scientific definitions are LINGUISTIC-ALLY more accurate than non-scientific ones. The precision of scientific definition serves the scientist's purpose, but it is in no way related to human language; it is no part of linguistics to 'tidy up' language by making it more 'scientific' in this way.

Bloomfield's theory loses its force when we realise how many of the relevant predisposing factors are unknown and unknowable. A more workable theory might seem to be one that defines meaning WHOLLY in terms of the observable stimulus and response. This is behaviourism of a kind that some psychologists favour, a kind that can be demonstrated in the laboratory with rats and other creatures responding in precise ways to certain clear and precise stimuli. The theory is limited to observables, and nothing is to be said about the internal structure of the organism. (This results from our ignorance about neuro-physiology – we are scientifically restricted to external behaviour and outside events.)

The question is whether this model can be applied to human language. Can we propose a theory in which in relation to speech the human being (a) is presented with a stimulus and (b) produces a response? According to B. F. Skinner we can indeed. His theory allows, however, as it must, that the same stimulus may produce different responses. This is accounted for in terms of REINFORCEMENT in which responses are partially conditioned by previous experiences, a notion similar to Bloomfield's predisposing factors.

The theory collapses into triviality when we realise that it is almost never the case that particular, present, observable stimuli produce specific linguistic responses. There is a wellknown and amusing passage in a review by Chomsky of Skinner's most relevant book. Here he discusses the possibility that on seeing a picture someone may say 'Dutch'. We thus have the stimulus (the picture), and the (linguistic) response. But Chomsky points out that in fact a whole variety of responses are possible including, 'Clashes with the wallpaper', or, 'Remember our camping trip last summer'. The variety of responses can only be explained if it is argued that the controlling stimuli are also different, that the response is not determined solely by the sight of the picture, but that we must take into account all the features of reinforcement. There is now a major difficulty – we cannot establish precisely what the controlling stimuli are except by working back to them from the responses. Since the whole point of the theory is that the responses are, in principle at least, predictable from the stimuli, the theory now becomes vacuous, since in practice the stimuli can be identified only from the responses. Thus there is no possibility of prediction and no scientific explanation at all.

3.4 *Linguistic relativity*

Part of the difficulty in relating language to the external world may arise from the fact that the way in which we see the world is to some degree dependent on the language we use. Since we categorise the objects of our experience with the aid of language, it may be the case that learning about the world and learning about language are activities that cannot be separated and that therefore 'our' world is partly determined by our language. Indeed Malinowski argued that primitive people have names only for those things that stand out for them from an otherwise 'undifferentiated world'. From a confused mass of experience, so to speak, they pick out by words those parts that are relevant to them.

Some scholars have taken a fairly extreme position on this. Edward Sapir, for instance, suggested that the world in which we live 'is to a large extent unconsciously built up on the language habits of the group'. His view was expanded and explained by Whorf and became known as the 'Sapir–Whorf hypothesis'. Whorf argued that we are unaware of the background character of our language, just as we are unaware of the presence of air until we begin to choke, and that if we look at other languages we come to realise that a language does not merely voice ideas, but that it is 'the shaper of ideas' and that we 'dissect nature along lines laid down by our native languages'. This leads him to a 'new principle of relativity which holds that all observers are not led by the same physical evidence to the same picture of the universe, unless their linguistic backgrounds are similar or in some way can be calibrated'.

In one article Whorf produces evidence of several kinds for his view. First, he suggests that there is no division in reality corresponding to English nouns and verbs. For why do we use nouns for *lightning, spark, wave, eddy, pulsation, flame, storm, phase, cycle, spasm, noise, emotion*? In the American Indian language Hopi all events of brief duration (mostly included in the English nouns above) are represented by verbs. In another American Indian language there is no noun/verb distinction at all; instead of 'There is a house' the form is (in translation) 'A house occurs' or better 'It houses'. Secondly, as we have already noted (2.1), Hopi has one word for insect, pilot and plane while Eskimo has three words for snow. We could add that some forms of Arabic have a large number of words (reputedly a hundred) for 'camel'. Thirdly, Whorf argued, their language shows that the Hopi have no notion of time. The only distinction they make is between what is subjective and what objective, the subjective including both the future and everything that is 'mental'. No distinction, moreover, is made (in the language and, therefore, by the Hopi themselves) between distance in time and distance in place.

It is not clear whether Sapir and Whorf thought that the 'shape' of the world was totally determined by our language, i.e. that without language it has no shape at all. Such an extreme interpretation is untenable for the same kind of reason as is the nominalist view of words as mere names of things. For if language classifies and categorises experience it must do so on the basis of some language-independent characteristic of that experience. In some sense, then, there is a world that we must share irrespective of the language we use. Moreover, unless there is some recognisable non-linguistic world of experience it is difficult to see how we could either learn a language or use it with our neighbours consistently.

Whorf's arguments as they stand are not wholly convincing. If we do not have the 'same picture of the universe' as the speakers of other languages, we nevertheless have a picture that can be related to and in some degree 'mapped upon' the picture that others have. That this is so is proved by the fact that we can investigate other languages (as Whorf did!), and that we can translate. It may well be that we can never totally absorb or understand the 'world' of other languages, but it is clear enough that we can obtain a very fair understanding of them. This we could not do if the pictures were totally different. Similarly, we often meet difficulties in translation, but we never totally fail to translate from one language to another. There may be no exact equivalence, but languages are never totally different.

Much of Whorf's argument, moreover, is invalid in that he argues from certain formal observable grammatical characteristics to a 'model of the Universe'. The Hopi's model is for him based largely upon the verbal system. But by a similar argument we could argue that English too has no concept of time. Let us look briefly at the English tense system (for more detail see Palmer 1974). Formally English has two tenses only, past and present as in *love* and *loved*. All other so-called tenses are composite forms involving auxiliary verbs, *was loving, will love*, etc.; these are not strictly part of the 'basic' tense system (and in this sense English has no future tense). Moreover, the 'past' tense is not semantically simply a matter of past time reference. The past tense may refer to past time as in *I went there yesterday*, but it is also used for 'unreality' as in *If I went tomorrow, I should see him* or *I wish I went there every day*. (It is no explanation, incidentally, to say that these are 'conditional' or 'subjunctive' forms rather than past tense. For the forms are the same as those of the past tense, and if the term 'past' seems misleading if applied to both, we could refer to them all as forms of 'tense 2'. Notice that even the highly irregular form *went* is used equally for past tense and unreality – it would be a remarkable coincidence if this were both past tense and conditional or subjunctive and not simply 'past tense' or 'tense 2'.) It has been actually suggested (by M. Joos) that English does not have a past tense, but a 'remote' tense to indicate what is remote in time or remote in reality. This makes English rather more like Hopi, and it is easy to see that, if English had been an American Indian language, it could have been used as an example of a language in which time relations are not distinguished. But few of us would believe that English speakers fail to make such time distinctions. It is clear that the grammatical structure of a language tells us little about our way of thinking about the world.

4

LEXICAL STRUCTURE

In this chapter we shall approach the problem of meaning from
the point of view of sense relations. We shall begin with some
familiar, traditional categories and then introduce some new
ones. Finally, we shall consider how such relations can be
handled within a 'structural' framework.

4.1 *Synonymy*

SYNONYMY is used to mean 'sameness of meaning'. It is obvious
that for the dictionary-maker many sets of words have the
same meaning; they are synonymous, or are synonyms of one
another. This makes it possible for them to define *gala* as
festivity or *mavis* as *thrush*, though there is little use in this
method if neither word is known to the reader, e.g. if *hoatzin*
is defined as *stink-bird*; or *neve* as *firn*. Of course, dictionaries
seldom rely solely on synonymy, but add descriptive details
to enlighten the reader.

It has often been suggested that English is particularly rich
in synonyms for the historical reason that its vocabulary has
come from two different sources, from Anglo Saxon on the
one hand and from French, Latin and Greek on the other.
Since English is considered to be a Germanic language from
a historical point of view, with Anglo-Saxon as an earlier stage
of its development, the 'Anglo-Saxon' words are often considered to be 'native' while those from French, Latin or Greek
are 'foreign', 'borrowed' from these languages. But the terms
'native' and 'foreign' are misleading. For whatever their
origins, most of the words are an essential and wholly natural
part of the English language; moreover, even some of the
'native' words may well have been 'borrowed' from some other

language at some time in the more remote past. Unfortunately, there are often moves to remove the 'foreign' element from languages. Frenchmen deplore 'Franglais' (the English words that are now common in colloquial French), while the Welsh spend time and scholarship to find substitutes for the 'English' words in the language, though they are quite happy to retain the 'Latin' words that entered an earlier form of the language at the time of the Roman Empire.

Nevertheless, it is true that there are pairs of 'native' and 'foreign' words. Thus we have *brotherly* and *fraternal, buy* and *purchase, world* and *universe,* and many others. The 'native' words are often shorter and less learned; four-letter words (in the quite literal sense) are mostly from Anglo-Saxon. There are examples too of triples, one 'native', one from French, one directly from Latin – *kingly, royal, regal* (though with this set it is the word of French origin, *royal,* that is today in more common usage).

It can, however, be maintained that there are no real synonyms, that no two words have exactly the same meaning. Indeed it would seem unlikely that two words with exactly the same meaning would both survive in a language. If we look at possible synonyms there are at least five ways in which they can be seen to differ.

First, some sets of synonyms belong to different dialects of the language. For instance, the term *fall* is used in the United States and in some western counties of Britain where others would use *autumn.* The works of dialectologists are full of examples like these. They are especially interested in the words to do with farming; depending where you live you will say *cowshed, cowhouse* or *byre, haystack, hayrick* or *haymow.* Even the domestic *tap* is either a *faucet* or a *spigot* in most of the United States. But these groups of words are of no interest at all for semantics. Their status is no different from the translation-equivalents of, say, English and French. It is simply a matter of people speaking different forms of the language having different vocabulary items.

Secondly, there is a similar situation, but a more problematic one, with the words that are used in different 'styles' or 'registers'. *A nasty smell* might be, in the appropriate setting, *an obnoxious effluvium* or *an 'orrible stink*. The former is, of course, jocularly very 'posh', and the latter colloquial. Similar trios (though not with quite the same stylistic characteristics, but differing rather in degrees of formality) are *gentleman, man* and *chap, pass away, die* and *pop off*. These are more difficult to deal with because there is a far less clear distinction between the styles than between the geographically defined dialects. We do not normally pass from one dialect to another, but we can within a single conversation change our style, and in particular, can change the vocabulary items to achieve different effects. The problem is, then, whether a change of style should be treated as a change from one 'language' to another or as a change within a single language. If the former, then stylistic synonyms are of no more interest than the dialectal synonyms or equivalent words in English or French. If the latter, we have to say that stylistic differences can be semantic. There is some plausibility in the view that, if we switch from style to style to achieve effect, this is a semantic feature. But there is a major objection to this. In changing style we may change not only the vocabulary, but also the grammar and the phonology, and it is difficult to incorporate stylistic differences as part of a phonological or grammatical system. It is simpler to handle them in terms of different but related 'languages', like the dialects. If this is applied to stylistic synonyms we shall not include them within semantics, but leave style as a matter for a separate investigation.

Thirdly, as we saw in 2.4, some words may be said to differ only in their emotive or evaluative meanings. The remainder of their meaning, their 'cognitive' meaning, remains the same. Examples were *statesman/politician, hide/conceal*; a further trio is *thrifty, economical, stingy*, and there is the related problem of the meaning of words such as *fascist* and *liberal*. Such words are often discussed in detail in books on semantics. They are, of course, interesting in the way in which they are used for persuading or influencing others, for propaganda, etc.

Nevertheless, it is a mistake to attempt to separate such emotive
or evaluative meaning from the 'basic' 'cognitive' meaning of
words for three reasons. First, as I have already argued, it is
not easy to establish precisely what cognitive meaning is, and
certainly not reasonable to attempt to define such meaning in
terms of reference to physical properties. In particular we
should notice that in this sense many verbs and adjectives will
have little or no cognitive meaning. Secondly, there are words
in English that are used PURELY for evaluative purposes, most
obviously the adjectives *good* and *bad*, but it is not normally
assumed that they have no cognitive meaning. Such words are
of interest to moral philosophers, but should not, I believe,
have any special place in linguistics. Thirdly, we make all
kinds of judgments and do not merely judge in terms of 'good'
and 'bad'. We judge size and use the appropriate terms –
giant/dwarf, *mountain/hill*, etc., and we make other kinds of
judgments in our choice of words. The meaning of words is not
simply a matter of 'objective' facts; a great deal of it is 'subjective' and we cannot clearly distinguish between the two.

Fourthly, some words are collocationally restricted (see 5.2),
i.e. they occur only in conjunction with other words. Thus
rancid occurs with *bacon* or *butter*, *addled* with *eggs* or *brains*.
This does not seem to be a matter of their meaning, but of the
company they keep. It could, perhaps, be argued that these
are true synonyms – differing only that they occur in different
environments. But, on the other hand, as we shall see shortly,
some scholars have actually thought that the test of synonyms
is whether they occur in identical environments!

Fifthly, it is obviously the case that many words are close
in meaning, or that their meanings overlap. There is, that is
to say, a loose sense of synonymy. This is the kind of synonymy
that is exploited by the dictionary maker. For *mature* (adjective), for instance, possible synonyms are *adult, ripe, perfect,
due*. For *govern* we may suggest *direct, control, determine,
require*, while *loose* (adjective) will have an even larger set –
inexact, free, relaxed, vague, lax, unbound, inattentive, slack,
etc. If we look for the synonyms for each of these words them-

selves, we shall have a further set for each and shall, of course, get further and further away from the meaning of the original word. Dictionaries, unfortunately (except the very large ones), tell us little about the connections between words and their defining synonyms or between the synonyms themselves.

It would be useful if we had some way of testing synonymy. One way, perhaps, is substitution – substituting one word for another. It has been suggested that true or total synonyms are mutually interchangeable in all their environments. But it is almost certainly the case that there are no total synonyms in this sense; indeed this would seem to be a corollary of the belief that no two words have exactly the same meaning. What we shall find, of course, is that some words are interchangeable in certain environments only, e.g. that *deep* or *profound* may be used with *sympathy* but only *deep* with *water*, that a *road* may be *broad* or *wide* but an *accent* only *broad*. But this will give us little measure of synonymy or of similarity of meaning; it will merely indicate the collocational possibilities, and these do not seem necessarily to be always closely related to nearness of meaning.

Another possibility is to investigate the 'opposites' (to be discussed in 4.5). Thus *superficial* is to be contrasted with both *deep* and *profound*, but *shallow* is, for the most part, in contrast only with *deep*. Perhaps the fact that two words appear to have the same antonyms is a reason for treating them as synonyms, but the examples we have just discussed show that we shall again arrive at the words that are interchangeable in certain environments, for it is precisely in the context in which *deep* and *profound* are interchangeable that they have the antonym *superficial*.

Finally, I must consider the term for 'connotation', for synonyms are often said to differ only in their connotations. This is not, in my view, a very useful term. It often refers to emotive or evaluative meaning, which I have argued is not usefully distinguished from cognitive meaning. It is also used to refer to stylistic or even dialectal differences or even to the small differences that are found in near-synonyms. But there is a further rather interesting use. It is sometimes suggested that words become associated with certain characteristics of the items to which they refer. Thus *woman* has the connotation 'weak' and *pig* the connotation 'dirty'. Such connotations were the subject of Osgood's investigations (1.5). Strictly, however, this is not a matter of the meaning of words or even of meaning in general. It rather indicates that people (or some people) believe that women are weak and pigs dirty. It is true that people will change names in order to avoid such connotations, and there is a natural process of change with taboo words such as those mentioned in 1.4. Because the word is associated with a socially distasteful subject, it becomes distasteful itself, and another word, a 'euphemism', takes its place. But the process is, of course, unending since it is essentially the object and not the word that is unpleasant. Words even become taboo when the distasteful object is referred to by the word in a different sense (whether it is homonymous or polysemous – see 4.2). Thus we are unwilling to talk of *intercourse* to mean social or commercial relationships, and it has been often pointed out that it is for similar reasons that in America the male domestic fowl is a *rooster*.

There are two phenomena that are sometimes handled under synonymy that have not yet been considered in this section. The first is context-dependent synonymy where two items appear to be synonymous in a particular context. Examples (taken from J. Lyons, though I am not presenting Lyons' arguments) are *dog* and *bitch* in *My — has just had pups* and *buy* and *get* in *I'll go to the shop and — some bread*. But this does not seem to be an argument for the synonymy of the words. On the contrary they are related in terms of hyponymy (see 4.4), one term being more specific than the other. The context, however, supplies the specific information that is lacking in one of the examples – having pups indicates that dog is female, going to the shop suggests that the bread is to be bought. But this is not part of the meaning. The dog might not be female (remarkable though it would be), and I might steal the bread. The fact that information can be gleaned from

the context does not affect the meaning of items. For consider
the book and *the red book*. These could well be contextually
synonymous (if we had already mentioned a red book – or,
non-linguistically, if there was one, red, book before us). Yet
we should not wish to say that these have the same meaning.
The second kind of 'synonymy' is that between *bull* and *male
adult bovine animal*. The test of interchangeability would rule
these out completely as synonymous, for one would hardly say
There is a male bovine animal in the field, even though in some
sense the two items seem to have the same meaning. But this
is not a 'natural' linguistic phenomenon; it is created by the
linguist or lexicographer for the purposes of definition and
paraphrase. It relates, moreover, more to componential analysis (4.7) than to synonymy.

4.2 *Polysemy and homonymy*
Sameness of meaning is not very easy to deal with but there
seems nothing inherently difficult about difference of meaning.
Not only do different words have different meanings; it is also
the case that the same word may have a set of different meanings. This is POLYSEMY; such a word is POLYSEMIC. Thus the
dictionary will define the word *flight* in at least the following
ways: 'passing through the air', 'power of flying', 'air journey',
'unit of the Air Force', 'volley', 'digression', 'series of steps'.
Yet there are problems even with this apparently simple concept.

First, we cannot clearly distinguish whether two meanings
are the same or different and, therefore, determine exactly
how many meanings a word has. For a meaning is not easily
delimited and so distinguished from other meanings. Consider
the verb *eat*. The dictionary will distinguish the 'literal' sense
(see below) of taking food and the derived meanings of 'use up'
and 'corrode' and we should, perhaps, treat these as three
different meanings. But we can also distinguish between eating
meat and eating soup, the former with a knife and fork and the
latter with a spoon. Moreover, we can talk about drinking
soup as well as eating it. In one of its senses, then, *eat* corres-

ponds to *drink*. The problem, however, is to decide whether this represents a distinct meaning of *eat*; for an alternative solution is that the meaning of *eat* merely overlaps that of *drink*, but that each covers a wide semantic 'area' (a great deal of which does not overlap). If we decide, however, that there are two meanings of *eat*, we may then ask whether eating jelly is the same thing as eating toffee (which involves chewing) or eating sweets (which involves sucking). Clearly we eat different types of food in different ways, and, if we are not careful, we shall decide that the verb *eat* has a different meaning with every type of food that we eat. The moral is that we ought not to look for all possible differences of meaning, but to look for sameness of meaning as far as we can, and that there is no clear criterion of either difference or sameness.

Secondly, we may ask whether we can make any general remarks about differences of meaning. Are regular types of difference found in the meaning of various words? One of the most familiar kinds of relationship between meanings is that of METAPHOR where a word appears to have both a 'literal' meaning and one or more 'transferred' meanings. The most striking set of examples is found with the words for parts of the body, *hand*, *foot*, *face*, *leg*, *tongue*, *eye*, etc., for we speak of the *hands* and *face* of a clock, the *foot* of a bed or of a mountain, the *leg* of a chair or table, the *tongue* of a shoe, the *eye* of a needle or a potato. Intuitively it is clear enough which is the literal sense, and our intuitions are supported by the fact that the whole set of words applies only to the body; only some of them can be transferred to the relevant object – the clock has no legs, the bed no hands, the chair no tongue, etc.

Metaphor is, however, fairly haphazard. It may seem obvious that *foot* is appropriate to mountains, or *eye* to needles, but a glance at other languages shows that it is not. In French the needle does not have an eye, and in many languages (e.g. the Ethiopian languages or some of those of North America) the mountain does not have a foot. Moreover, in English *eye* is used with a variety of other meanings, e.g. the centre of a hurricane or a spring of water, which are not so obviously related semantically to the organ of sight, yet it is not used for the centre of a flower or an identation, though these might seem intuitively to be reasonable candidates for the extension of the meaning.

There are some other kinds of 'transference' that are more 'regular'. Thus many adjectives may be used either literally for the quality referred to or with the transferred meaning of being the source of the quality. Thus a person may be *sad* and a book may be *sad*, while a coat may be *warm* in the two senses (either that it is of a certain degree of temperature or that it keeps one warm). The language recognises the difference of meaning in that we cannot say *John is as sad as the book he was reading*. This is similar to the traditional grammarian's concept of ZEUGMA (*She was wearing a white dress and a smile on her face*), for in each case one word co-occurs with two other words and these two each require the first to have a different meaning, and this the language does not allow. Similarly, many nouns have a concrete and an abstract sense. Thus we may compare *The score of the symphony is on the table* and *The score of the symphony is difficult to follow*. Notice once again that we cannot say *The score is on the table and difficult to follow*. Similar contrasts hold for *thesis, book, bible*, etc.

Thirdly, there is the problem that if one form has several meanings, it is not always clear whether we shall say that this is an example of polysemy (that there is one word with several meanings) or of HOMONYMY (that there are several words with the same shape). For instance we noted earlier that the dictionary treats *flight* as a single (polysemic) word. But it recognises no less than five words (i.e. five homonyms) for *mail* – 'armour', 'post', 'payment', 'halfpenny' and 'spot'. The dictionary has to decide whether a particular item is to be handled in terms of polysemy or homonymy, because a polysemic item will be treated as a single entry, while a homonymous one will have a separate entry for each of the homonyms. This does not mean, of course, that we can decide between polysemy and homonymy by merely consulting the dictionary, for the decisions by the dictionary maker often seem to be quite arbitrary.

There is some complication in the fact that we do not make the same distinctions in writing and speech. Thus *lead* (metal) and *lead* (dog's lead) are spelt in the same way, but pronounced differently, while *site* and *sight*, *rite* and *right* are spelt differently but pronounced in the same way. For the former the term HOMOGRAPHY may be used, for the latter HOMOPHONY. Curiously there are some homonyms and homophones that are also (very nearly) antonyms, e.g. *cleave* 'part asunder' and *cleave* 'unite' and *raise* and *raze*.

The problem, however, is to decide when we have polysemy and when we have homonymy. Given that we have a written form with two meanings, are we to say that it is one word with different meanings (polysemy) or two different words with the same shape (homonymy)?

In general the dictionaries base their decision upon etymology. If it is known that identical forms have different origins they are treated as homonymous and given separate entries; if it is known that they have one origin, even if they have different meanings, they are treated as polysemic and given a single entry in the dictionary. This is, however, far from satisfactory, for the history of a language does not always reflect accurately its present state. For instance, we should not usually relate *pupil* (=student) with the *pupil* of the eye, or the *sole* of a shoe with the fish *sole*. Yet historically they are from the same origin, and as such are examples of polysemy. Yet in the language of today they are pairs of unrelated words, i.e. homonyms. On the other side we find, as we have seen, that we speak of the *hands* and *face* of a clock, the *foot* of a bed, the *tongue* of a shoe, as well as using the same terms for parts of the body, and similarly have the word *ear* used of the *ear* of corn. These would all seem to be examples of metaphor and, so, of polysemy. Yet the etymologists tell us that the *ear* of corn is in no way related (historically) to the *ear* of the body. Historically, then, they are homonyms. But most people today would regard them as the same word with different meanings, i.e. as examples of polysemy. There are other examples – *corn* (=grain) and *corn* on the foot, *meal* (=repast) and *meal* (=flour), each of which has a different etymology. But are they different words for us today? I do not, of course, claim that we can always distinguish polysemy and homonymy in our present day language. I only wish to show that history can be misleading.

Curiously, a difference of spelling does not always indicate a difference of origin. Thus even what are today homophones may be derived from the same original form. Examples are *metal* and *mettle*, *flour* and *flower*. These pose real problems for the semanticist. For if he relies on his historical knowledge, they are the same word, merely examples of polysemy, even though they are spelt differently. Yet this is odd. Can we consider words that are spelt differently to be the 'same' word? Yet we find that difference of spelling does not guarantee difference of origin. Does the dictionary maker then treat these as different words because they are spelt differently, or as the same word because they have a single origin? In practice he usually (but not always) allows the spelling difference to decide, because he needs to keep words in their alphabetical position.

A second way of attempting to establish polysemy rather than homonymy is to look for a central meaning or a core of meaning. This is possible where we have examples of metaphor or of the 'transferred' meanings we noted for *sad* and *score*. But in general it is very difficult to decide whether there is any central or core meaning. It is obvious enough why *key* is used not only for key of the door, but also for a translation or a keystone (one 'unlocks', the other 'locks'), but it is by no means easy to see why it is used for the keys of a piano and, therefore, not at all clear that this is an example of polysemy. Nor is there any obvious relation between *air* 'atmosphere' and the meanings of 'manner' and 'tune'. With verbs the problem is often even greater. *Charge* is used of electricity, of charging expenses, of a cavalry attack and of an accusation. These are quite far apart in their meanings. Can we discover a central or core meaning?

If we look at what has happened in history we see why the problem has arisen. Words change their meaning in quite surprising ways. Thus *arrive* is derived from Latin *ripa* 'a shore', and originally meant 'reach shore', while *rival* comes from Latin *rivus* 'a stream', rivals originally being people who shared the same stream. With such changes it is not surprising that meanings of *charge* should have so diverged – its earlier meaning is 'load', and it is related to *car* and even, in a less direct fashion, to *cargo*.

Where a word is polysemic it will, naturally, have a variety of synonyms each corresponding to one of its meanings. It will often also have a set of antonyms. Thus *fair* may be used with (1) *hair*, (2) *skin*, (3) *weather*, (4) *sky*, (5) *judgment*, (6) *tackle*. The obvious antonyms would seem to be (1) *dark*, (2) *dark*, (3) *foul*, (4) *cloudy*, (5) *unfair*, (6) *foul*. (It is also used with *work* or *performance*, but there it is a middle term, 'neither good nor bad' and has, thus, no antonym.) It can be seen that *fair* with *hair* and *fair* with *skin* have the same antonym (*dark*), and so do *fair* with *weather* and *fair* with *tackle* (*foul*). We might be tempted to say that where the antonym is the same we have polysemy, and that difference of antonym implies homonymy. But this will suggest that *fair* with *weather* is more like *fair* with *tackle* than *fair* with *sky*. Intuitively, *sky* is more closely related to *weather* and *tackle* to *judgment*, but the antonyms do not provide evidence for this.

Finally, there may sometimes be formal reasons for recognising polysemy. Ullmann quotes the French word *poli* which means polished either in the literal or the transferred sense. These would seem to be a clear example of homonymy, and historically they have a single origin. But in the literal sense the word is linked with *dépolir* ('take polish off') and *polissage* ('polishing'), while in the other sense it goes with *impoli* ('unpolished' or 'impolite') and *politesse* ('politeness'). This seems to suggest that there are two different words that belong to two different related sets.

Notice, finally, that multiplicity of meaning is not confined to the words of the dictionary. It is also found with grammatical elements – the English past tense has two different meanings (3.4). So do some prefixes; *in-* usually means 'not', but this is not so in *inflammable*. (This word has led, through misunderstanding resulting from the ambiguity of the prefix, to some unfortunate accidents, and on the advice of Whorf it has become the practice in the USA to use the invented word *flammable* instead.) There is similar ambiguity in syntax. Familiar examples are *The old men and women* and *Visiting relatives can be a nuisance*. Both can be analysed differently in syntax with accompanying difference of meaning. Multiplicity of meaning is a very general characteristic of language.

4.3 *Incompatibility*

So far we have discussed the fact that different words may have the same meaning and that the same words may have different meanings. It is obvious that different words may have different meanings. Simple difference of meaning is itself not of great interest, but only where the differences are in some way related.

I shall begin with a brief discussion of what is known on the FIELD THEORY of semantics. This derives very largely from de Saussure's notion of VALUE. He pointed out that a knight on a chess board is a knight not because of any inherent quality (shape, size, etc.), but because of what it can do in relation to the other pieces on the board. He stressed this relational aspect of language, saying that there were 'only differences and no positive terms'. For instance, he argued that *sheep* in English has a different value from *mouton* in French because English has also the word *mutton*. Similarly plural in Sanskrit has a different value from plural in French (or English), because in Sanskrit it belongs to the three-term system singular, dual, plural, while in French it belongs to a two-term system of singular and plural only. He further argued that if we consider synonyms such as *dread, fear, be afraid*, we can say that if one of these did not exist its 'content' would go to one of the others; in other words, the field of 'fearing' is divided among three verbs (or more, of course, in actual fact), but if one were absent it would be divided between two only.

The most famous example of field theory is that of J. Trier who compared the field of the 'intellectual' aspect of the German of around 1200 with that of around 1300. (For a detailed discussion the reader should refer to Ullmann's *Semantics*.) In the earlier period the field was divided into *kunst* and *list*, the former referring to courtly qualities and the second to non-courtly skills. The term *wîsheit* was used to cover the whole. In the later period, however, the field was divided into three – *wîsheit* 'religious experience', *kunst* 'knowledge' and *wizzen* 'art' (one new term, one term lost and *wîsheit* now only one part, not the whole).

Trier's example compared a language at two different periods. We can also compare two languages to see the way in which they divide up a particular field. An often quoted example is that of colour terms. The Danish linguist, L. Hjelmslev, argued that we could compare the colour system of English and literary Welsh in the diagram:

	gwyrdd
green	
blue	glas
grey	
brown	llwydd

There are many other similar examples. E. A. Nida discusses in terms of 'class', the words in a Mexican language for noise; there are six 'noise' words referring to children yelling, people talking loudly, people arguing (or turkeys gobbling), people talking angrily, increasing noise and funeral noise. Similarly he noted in Mayan three words for searching, (a) to select good from bad, (b) search in a disorderly way, (c) search in an orderly way, and in Shilluk (Africa) three 'break' words, one for breaking sticks, etc., one for string, one for eggs. We can add to this list a number of familiar classes, the metals *iron*, *copper*, etc., the mammals *lion*, *tiger*, or types of motor car and so on.

In all these examples we have a list of words referring to items of a particular class dividing up a semantic 'field'. But in almost all cases a relevant point is that the words are IN-COMPATIBLE. We cannot say *This is a red hat* and of the same object *This is a green hat*. Nor shall we allow a creature to be described both as a lion and as an elephant. Sentences with incompatible terms will thus contradict each other. Sometimes incompatibility is a reflection of a clear (and, perhaps, even scientific) definition in the world of experience. Lions and elephants are distinct species and copper and iron different metals. But this is not wholly relevant. What IS relevant is that the terms themselves are incompatible, even if there may be no clear distinction in the world. Consider, for example, the colour terms *red* and *orange*. There is no clear dividing line in the spectrum between these two classes (and if a scientist decides to make a strict cut-off point in terms of wavelength, that is not relevant to ordinary language), yet we would never agree that a particular object was red and at the same time orange (I am not, of course, concerned with a combination of the two colours). We might even describe it as red one day and orange the next, yet we would still never admit that it was both red and orange. *Red* and *orange* are incompatible terms.

It may be the case that in some areas there is overlap. This may be true of the lists quoted from Nida but, in general, terms in systems of this kind acquire their 'value', as de Saussure said, from their contrastive relations with the others, and are incompatible.

The basic characteristic of the items in these classes is their incompatibility. Moreover, they are 'unordered'; that is to say there is no natural way, as far as their meaning is concerned, of arranging them in any kind of order – and if we wanted to list them we should, therefore, probably do so in alphabetic

order. Admittedly, the scientist will have a framework for the
classification of metals or mammals, but that is a different
matter; there is no way in which, in terms of an obvious meaning characteristic, we can arrange *elephant, giraffe, rhinoceros*.
But there are some groups of words that seem to have some
'order'. The days of the week and the months of the year form
sets of incompatible items since we cannot say *This month is
November and it is also March*. But they also have sequential
relations such that Sunday comes immediately before Monday
– *Sunday is the day before Monday*, etc. Similarly, measure-
ments such as *inch, foot, yard* can be put in order, starting
from the smallest one. The numbers *one, two, three*, etc., are
another obvious example. Nida quotes a rather different counting system from a Brazilian language in which the terms are
(roughly translated) 'none', 'one or two', 'three or four', 'many'.
But we must be careful here. In mathematics we have sequences
other than *one, two, three* . . .; we have also *two, four, six,
eight* . . ., *one, four, nine, sixteen* (squares) . . ., and addicts of
IQ tests will know that dozens of others can be invented. Not
all of this can be a matter of semantics, but where do we draw
the line?

We can sometimes provide a much more sophisticated
'scientific analysis of some of these fields than the language
itself seems to provide. The colour terms, for instance, are
strictly, no more than an unordered set of incompatible terms.
Yet Hjelmslev placed them in an order by setting them along
the dimension of wavelength. This is not reflected in the
language. We have no adjective to say that *Red is more — than
orange* and *Orange is more — than yellow*, etc. The ordering
is not then reflected in English as is that of the days of the
week or the months of the year. But if we are to look for the
physical characteristics of colour, Hjelmslev's account says too
little rather than too much. Colour is not to be accounted for
in terms of a single dimension. It involves three variables. The
most obvious is that of hue, which can be measured in wavelengths and is seen in the spectrum or the rainbow. Another is
luminosity or brightness and a third saturation, the degree of

freedom from white. Thus *pink* differs from *red* mainly in that it has low saturation (it has a lot of white in it). We probably think of colour mainly as hue, but this may not be true of all societies. It has often been noted that Homer referred to the sea as 'wine-coloured', which is very odd if we think of its hue, but completely understandable if we think of its luminosity and saturation, which are very similar to those of a deep red wine.

It does not appear, however, that there is always a close relation between these physical features and the colour system of a particular language. Thus in a language of the Philippines, Hanunóo, described by H. C. Conklin, there are four basic colour terms that may be roughly translated 'black', 'white', 'red' and 'green'. But the distinctions between them are of three kinds. First, light and dark essentially distinguishes 'black' and 'white' (all light tints being 'white', but violet, blue, dark green, being 'black'). Secondly, the distinction between 'red' and 'green' is largely in terms of the fact that all living plants are green, even slimy but light brown bamboo shoots. Thirdly, a distinction is made in terms of deep indelible colours 'black' and 'red' versus the weaker 'white' and 'green'. It is clear that the colour system is not solely based upon the physical features of colour, but is partly determined by the cultural needs, the need, for instance, to distinguish living and dead bamboo, one 'green' the other 'red'.

Even in English colour words are not always used in ways that correspond to their scientific definition. The use of *green* has some similarity to that found in Hanunóo, since dried peas are green in colour, but would not be referred to as *green peas*, while *green* is often used of unripe fruit – it may seem odd, but I should be understood, if I referred to some greengages as being 'still green' and therefore inedible. Similarly (see 5.3), *white* is brown when relating to coffee, yellow when referring to wine and pink as applied to people. Nor should we say, I think, that the huntsmen are colour-blind when they refer to the bright red jackets as *pink*. Modern Welsh, more surprisingly, has colour terms corresponding to those of English (not the older system described by Hjelmslev), yet uses the word *glas* to refer to grass and other growing things, though *glas* otherwise translates English *blue*.

Considerations like these should make us wary of arranging colour words along scientific dimensions or of comparing the words of one language with those of another in terms of such dimensions. Their incompatibility is clear enough, but it is far less clear that they have any natural order.

4.4 *Hyponymy*

In the last section we discussed classes or sets of incompatible items. But there are also words that refer to the class itself. This involves us in the notion of INCLUSION in the sense that *tulip* and *rose* are included in *flower*, and *lion* and *elephant* in *mammal* (or perhaps *animal* – see below). Similarly *scarlet* is included in *red*. Inclusion is thus a matter of class membership.

Lyons' term for the relation is HYPONOMY. The 'upper' term is the SUPERORDINATE and the 'lower' term the HYPONYM. In the previous section we were concerned with members of a class with, that is to say, co-hyponyms. Yet oddly there is not always a superordinate term. Lyons' own work led him to observe that in Classical Greek there is a superordinate term to cover a variety of professions and crafts, 'carpenter', 'doctor', 'flute player', 'helmsman', 'shoemaker', etc., but none in English. The nearest possible term is *craftsman*, but that would not include *doctor*, *flute player* or *helmsman*. Similarly, and rather strangely, there is no superordinate term for all colour words, *red, blue, green, white,* etc.; the term *coloured* usually excludes *black* and *white* (and *grey* too), or else (used to refer to race), means 'non-white'.

The same term may appear in several places in the hierarchy. This is, of course, possible only if it is polysemic; in one of its meanings it may actually be superordinate to itself in another meaning (though we should usually avoid using both terms in the same context). Thus *animal* may be used (i) in contrast with *vegetable* to include birds, fishes, insects as well as mammals, (ii) in the sense of 'mammals' to contrast with birds, fishes and insects, to include both humans and beasts, (iii) in the sense of 'beast' to contrast with *human*. Thus it occurs three times in the hierarchical classification of nature. A diagram illustrates the point clearly:

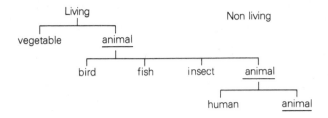

There is a similar situation with the word *dog*. The word *sheep* is used for all creatures of a certain species; it is the superordinate term of *ewe, lamb, ram*, etc. There are similar terms *pig* for *sow, boar, piglet* and *horse* for *stallion, mare, colt*, etc. But the superordinate term for dogs is *dog*, though *dog* is also the hyponym as distinct from *bitch*. Again a diagram will help:

We can, of course, avoid the ambiguity of *dog* by using the term *male*; thus *male dog* would be hyponym to contrast with *bitch*. We can also form hyponymous sets where no single-word hyponyms exist in English in a similar way, e.g. *giraffe, male giraffe, female giraffe, baby giraffe*. The terms *cattle* and *poultry* are a little odd in that, though they are superordinate, they are used only for plural reference (though, of course, we need the superordinate term quite commonly for the plural). Thus, though we may say *Those are cattle* to include *Those are cows, Those are bulls*, we have no single term to put in the

frame *That is a* —. The most likely term here would be *cow*.
(I personally would find it difficult to say *That is a cow* of a bull,
but would not be unhappy with the definition of a bull as *a
male cow*.) With *poultry* the situation seems to vary according
to interest and dialect. The terms *cock* (or *cockerel* and, in
America, *rooster*), *hen* and *chick* are available, but many people
use *hen* or *chicken* as the superordinate term, though would
not, I suspect, ever wish to refer to the male bird as a *hen*. In
my own 'native' dialect there is no problem – the superordinate
term is *fowl*.

As we might expect, hyponymy relations vary from language
to language. We have seen one example – that Greek has a
superordinate term to include a variety of occupations. Another
example is that in German 'potato' *Kartoffel* is not included
among 'vegetables' *Gemüse*.

Hyponymy involves the logical relationship of ENTAILMENT.
This is a more precise characterisation of the relation of
'follows from' that was mentioned in the discussion of Bierwisch's examples in 2.3. To say that one sentence entails
another is to say that if the first sentence is true, the second is
(on logical grounds) also true. To say *This is a tulip* entails
This is a flower, and *This is scarlet* entails *This is red*. Similarly
There are two boys entails *There are two children*. In all such
examples a sentence containing the hyponym entails a sentence
containing the superordinate term. But if we have reference to
'all' the items (whether or not the term *all* actually occurs), the
reverse is the case. Thus *All flowers are lovely* entails *All tulips
are lovely* and *Children are a nuisance* entails *Boys are a
nuisance*, but not vice-versa.

4.5 *Antonymy*

The term ANTONYMY is used for 'oppositeness of meaning';
words that are opposite are ANTONYMS. Antonymy is often
thought of as opposite of synonymy, but the status of the two
are very different. For languages have no real need of true
synonyms, and, as we have seen, it is doubtful whether any
true synonyms exist. But antonymy is a regular and very

natural feature of language and can be defined fairly precisely. Yet, surprisingly, it is a subject that has often been neglected in books on semantics and it is not even usually given a place in dictionaries. However, there are different kinds of 'oppositeness' and we must clearly distinguish them.

To begin with, English abounds in pairs of words such as *wide/narrow*, *old/young*, *big/small*, etc. These, all of them adjectives, have in common the fact that they may be seen in terms of degrees of the quality involved. Thus a road may be *wide* or *very wide* and one road may be *wider* than another. We have, that is to say, gradation of width, age, size, etc., all indicated by such adjectives as these.

Sapir argued that we should handle all these words in terms of GRADABILITY. The comparative forms of the adjectives (those ending in *-er* or occurring with *more*) are EXPLICITLY graded, since to say that one road is wider than another, one boy is older than another or one book is bigger than another is to place them in a graded scale for comparison. Sapir went on to argue that although these comparative forms are preceded linguistically by the simple forms (i.e. formed from them by adding *-er* or *more*), they precede them logically in that *wide*, *old* and *big* can only be understood in terms of being wider, older, bigger than something – some norm or other. They are thus, said Sapir, IMPLICITLY graded antonyms.

Not only are these adjectives gradable, but they are graded against different norms according to the items being discussed. For instance, if I say that not many people were present, this might mean five or six if we were talking about an intimate party, but perhaps as many as twenty thousand if we were talking about the attendance at an important football match at Wembley. The norm is set by the object being described. A stripe on a dress may be wide if it is only two inches wide, but a road would have to be many yards wide before it could be so described. This accounts for the apparent paradoxes of a small elephant being bigger than a big mouse for *small* means 'small as elephants go' and *big* 'big as mice go'.

For most antonyms a set of relationships hold between the

comparative forms such that all of the following are mutually implied:

A is wider than B
B is narrower than A
A is less narrow than B
B is less wide than A

These are related both in terms of simple reversal with switch of antonyms, and the 'more' and 'less' relationship (again involving switch of antonyms). Not surprisingly, since antonyms are gradable, there are often intermediate terms. Thus we have not just *hot/cold*, but *hot/warm/cool/cold*, with the intermediate *warm* and *cool* forming a pair of antonyms themselves.

A further point is that in each pair one of the terms is the 'marked' term and the other 'unmarked' in that only one is used simply to ask about or describe the degree of the gradable quality. We say *How high is it? How wide is it? It is three feet high. It is four yards wide*, with no implication that it is either high or wide. But the other term of the pair is not so used – it is the 'marked term'. Thus *How low is it? How narrow is it?* imply that the object in question actually is low or narrow and we would not say (except jocularly) *It is three feet low* or *It is four yards narrow*. Notice also that the same member of the pair is used to form the nouns, *height* and *width*, which are equally neutral as compared with *lowness* and *narrowness*. In the English examples it is the 'larger' term that appears to be unmarked, but this does not appear to be a universal feature. Where English talks of a 'thickness gauge' Japanese talks of a 'thinness gauge'.

We may, perhaps, also include here pairs of the type *male/female, married/single, alive/dead*. These Lyons treats in term of COMPLEMENTARITY, the items being complementary to each other. Strictly these belong to the set of incompatible terms that were discussed in 4.3, but with one specific characteristic – that they are members of two-term sets instead of the multiple-term sets that we discussed there. But they are in some ways similar to our gradable antonyms. Both exhibit incompatibility. To say that something is wide is to say that it is not narrow. To say that someone is married is to say that he is not single. But there is one striking difference between the two types. With the pairs we have introduced it is also the case that to say something is NOT the one is to say that it is the other. If Peter is NOT married, he is single, and vice versa. This results, of course, from the fact that there are only two possibilities (it would not be the same with the multiple sets). With the gradable antonyms, in contrast, although there are only two terms, it is not the case that to say something is not (for instance) wide is to say that it is narrow, or that to say it is not narrow is to say that it is wide. The possibility of being neither wide nor narrow is left open.

An interesting point, however, is that there is no absolute distinction between these two types. We can treat *male/female, married/single, alive/dead* as gradable antonyms on occasions. Someone can be *very male* or *more married* and certainly *more dead than alive*. More obviously, some gradable antonyms have some characteristics of the dichotomous pairs:

(i) There are some pairs of adjectives, e.g. *honest/dishonest, obedient/disobedient, open/shut* that are gradable in terms of *more* and *less*, yet in which the denial of one is usually taken to assert the other. Thus though we may say *Bill is more honest than John, Bill isn't honest* implies that *Bill is dishonest* and *Bill isn't dishonest* implies that *Bill is honest*. These are, that is to say, explicitly gradable, but they are not usually treated as implicitly gradable.

(ii) Some pairs of antonyms are, in Sapir's terms, not 'symmetrically reversible'. That is to say the *more* and *less* relationship cannot be applied to them. An example is the pair *brilliant* and *stupid*, since *more brilliant* does not equal *less stupid* or *more stupid, less brilliant*. The terms, though gradable, also have an absolute value at one of the 'ends' of the scale.

4.6 *Relational opposites*

A quite different kind of 'opposite' is found with pairs of words which exhibit the reversal of a relationship between items (or

ARGUMENTS – see 6.3). Examples are *buy/sell, husband/wife*. If A sells to B, B buys from A; if A is B's husband, B is A's wife. Lyons suggests the term CONVERSENESS for these, but I am more concerned to point out their essentially relational characteristics, and would thus prefer RELATIONAL OPPOSITION.

There are several verbs that are pairs in this way – *buy/sell, lend/borrow, rent/let, own/belong to, give/receive*. There are also nouns – *husband/wife, fiancé/fiancée, parent/child, debtor/creditor*, and, possibly, *teacher/pupil*. A number of terms referring to spatial position also belong here – *above/below, in front of/behind, north of/south of*, etc. In grammar, too, active and passive exhibit relational opposition, for if A hits B, B is hit by A.

Relations are often characterised by logicians in terms of SYMMETRY, TRANSITIVITY and REFLEXIVITY. A relation is symmetric if it holds for the arguments (the related items) in both directions. If we have arguments a and b and a relation R, then a R b entails b R a. Obvious examples in English are *be married to* and *cousin*, for if John is married to Mary, Mary is married to John and if Bill is Fred's cousin, Fred is Bill's cousin. A relation is transitive if a R b and b R c entail a R c. Thus many of the spatial terms are transitive – if John is in front of Harry and Harry is in front of Bill, John is also in front of Bill. The same is true for *behind, above, below, north of, south of* and *inside*. This does not, of course, hold for *opposite*, which is symmetrical (if A is opposite B, B is opposite A), but not transitive. (It must be noted that *transitive* and *transivity* are used in a completely different sense in grammar – see 7.5.) A relation is reflexive if it relates an argument to itself, i.e. a R a. It can be exemplified by *equal* or *resemble* (*Four equals four, John resembles himself*). (These words are symmetrical and transitive too.) Reflexivity is, however, of little interest to us here, and will not be further discussed.

Kinship terms are especially interesting in a discussion of relational opposites for two reasons. In the first place many of them indicate not only the relationship, but the sex of the person concerned. Thus *father* is male parent, *daughter* the female child and so on. This blocks reversability. For to say that John is Sam's father does not entail that Sam is John's son – Sam could be his daughter. We therefore have pairs indicating the same relationship but a different sex – *father/mother, son/ daughter, uncle/aunt, nephew/niece.* There are also pairs of words that would be symmetrical were it not for their indication of sex. An example are *brother* and *sister.* It does not follow that if John is Sam's brother, Sam is John's brother (she might be his sister). Only a small number of terms in English do not indicate sex – *cousin* (which is symmetrical) and *parent* and *child* (together with grandparent and grandchild) which are not. Rare terms are available, though they are most used only by anthropologists in order to avoid sex reference – *spouse* for *husband/wife* and *sibling* for *brother/sister* (both are symmetrical). But there are no similar terms for *uncle/aunt, nephew/niece.* Secondly, whether a term is symmetrical or not is a matter of the language. Thus *be married to* is symmetrical in English, because like *spouse* it does not indicate sex. But in many languages a different term is used for husband and wife, quite often the active form of the verb for the husband and the passive term for the wife – John 'marries' Mary but Mary 'is married' to John. (In English *marry* and *be married to* are used for either partner, and so are both symmetrical, though they have different meanings.) Similarly, many languages have no symmetrical term *cousin*; the sex has to be indicated in these languages, or the precise relationship of the parents. There may be other complications too. The brother and sister relationship in some languages is bound up not only with the sex, but also the age of the child; thus if two girls are sisters, one is the 'elder sister', one the 'younger sister' of the other.

There are some other terms that are not strictly related as relational opposites, but nevertheless differ in spatial direction in some way. A most interesting pair (discussed by C. J. Fillmore) is *come* and *go.* *Come* is restricted in a way that *go* is not, in that it indicates direction towards the speaker or hearer. It is used, first, for simple direction towards speaker or hearer as in *Come to me* and *I'll come to you*. But, secondly, it is also used for direction towards speaker or hearer at the time of the relevant event, either in the past or the future (as well as the present) – *He came to me in London, I'll come to see you in Paris* (*when you get there*). Thirdly, it is used to refer to direction to a place at which the speaker or hearer is habitually found, even if he is not there at the relevant time, e.g. *Come to my office* (*though I shan't be there*), *I came to your house* (*but you were out*). In this third case *go* is also possible, *Go to my office, I went to your house*. Moreover, if the reference is to motion AWAY from the position of the relevant person, *go* would be much more normal. I could hardly say *Come to my office immediately*, if the person I am addressing is with me in some place other than my office, since the motion is then clearly away from me. Similarly we should not normally say *He left you at his house and came to yours* for again the motion is away from the relevant person. If there is no indication at all of the position of either hearer or speaker, *go* will be used. *Come* and *go* are not the only pair of verbs with these characteristics. *Bring* and *take* function in exactly the same way, with the additional meaning of 'carry'.

There are other pairs of words that seem to be related in similar ways. Thus *ask* expects *reply* and *offer, accept*. These are not examples of relational opposites, but of a temporal relationship. Moreover the relationship between the members of each pair is not the same. *Ask* and *offer* may 'expect' *reply* and *accept*, but the 'expectation' may be disappointed – there may be no reply or acceptance (though, for *offer*, there is also the term *refuse*). But *reply* and *accept* also 'presuppose' that there has been an act of asking or giving (see 8.4); this is a natural result of the temporal relationship.

Finally, it is worth noting that the 'true' gradable antonyms can be treated basically in terms of relational opposites. For we saw that *wide* can be seen as wider than the norm and that if a is wider than b, b is narrower than a. The comparative forms *wider* and *narrower* (the explicitly gradable forms) are thus relational opposites; they are, moreover, transitive (if a is wider than b and b is wider than c, a is wider than c), but not symmetrical or reflexive. Notice, however, that *as wide as*, *as narrow as*, etc., are symmetrical, transitive and reflexive.

4.7 *Components*

In the previous section of this chapter we have considered various semantic relationships, without generally trying to relate them (though we have just seen a connection between antonymy and relational opposites). A very different approach, it might seem at first sight, is analysis in terms of COMPONENTS – the total meaning of a word being seen in terms of a number of distinct elements or components of meaning. The notion of component does not introduce a further kind of relation; rather it purports to offer a theoretical framework for handling all the relations we have been discussing.

The idea that semantics could be handled in terms of components has been argued with the investigation of kinship terms. It was noted that in Spanish, for instance, the sex of the people involved is clearly marked – ending -*o* for male, -*a* for female as in:

tio	uncle	tia	aunt
hijo	son	hija	daughter
abuelo	grandfather	abuela	grandmother
hermano	brother	hermana	sister

English has no markers of sex, of course, though the ending -*ess* occurs in *baroness, tigress, lioness, duchess*, etc. But if we are concerned with semantics that is not particularly relevant. There is no reason why we should not attempt to classify the English kinship terms with reference to categories such as sex, even if the language does not mark these terms in the form of the words.

Sex therefore provides one set of components for kinship terms; generation differences and degrees of relationship provide two others. Thus for generation differences we need at least five generations which may be labelled g_1, g_2, g_3, g_4, g_5. Then *grandfather* is g_1, *father, uncle*, etc., g_2, *brother, cousin*, g_3, *son*, *niece* g_4, and *grandson* g_5. On such a system the 'ego' (the person for whom the relationships hold) is, obviously g_3. Of course we would need others to deal with *great grandfather*, etc. Degrees of relationship involve LINEALITY – DIRECT for *grandfather*, *father*, COLINEAL for *brother*, *uncle* (but with different generation) and ABLINEAL for *cousin*. Given these three sets of components all the English kinship terms can be handled. *Aunt* is thus female, g_2 and colineal, *cousin* male or female, g_3 and ablineal.

We can most easily recognise components where words can be set out in a diagrammatic form to represent some kind of 'proportional' relationship. In English (and the same is true of many other languages) there is a three-fold division with many words that refer to living creatures:

man	woman	child
bull	cow	calf
ram	ewe	lamb
boar	sow	piglet

Thus *bull* is to *cow* as *ram* is to *ewe* – or in mathematical terms *bull*:*cow* :: *ram*:*ewe*. In the light of relationships such as these we can abstract the components (male) and (female), (adult) and (non adult), plus (human), (bovine), (ovine) and (porcine). Strictly these examples do not distinguish (male) and (female) in full conjunction with (adult) and (non adult), since that would imply four possibilities and we only have three. But all four are to be found in:

man   woman   boy   girl

However, even with the other examples, it is more plausible to make both distinctions than to say that there are simply three possibilities – (male), (female) and (non adult).

Analysis of this kind (COMPONENTIAL ANALYSIS) allows us to provide definition for all these words in terms of a few components. Thus *boar* is (porcine), (male), (adult) and so on. There are, as we saw earlier, gaps in the system – there are no terms to distinguish between the male, female and the young with giraffes or rhinoceroses. Often the distinction is made by using a term taken from another set in conjunction with the generic one – *bull elephant, cow elephant* and *elephant calf*. Badgers are similarly *boars* and *sows* (though the young are presumably *cubs*); the male fox is a *dog* or *dog-fox*, but the female has a specific term *vixen*.

In many cases there is an appropriate word in the language to label the component. *Male* and *female* are obvious examples. But it would be a mistake to suppose that if we use such terms to define a common word that the resultant phrase is semantically identical with it. Thus *boar* is not the same as *male adult pig* (see 4.1); it is important to note that in the vocabulary of English we have words such as *boar*, whereas with *giraffe* we can only use the phrase *adult male giraffe*; the difference is relevant to the semantic structure of English.

Such labels are not, however, always readily available. We have noted the semantic relationship:

come   go
bring   take

We noted that *come* is to *go* as *bring* is to *take* and we could therefore distinguish components X and Y and A and B such that *come* is XA and *go* XB, *bring* YA and *take* YB. But what could be the names of these components? It is difficult to provide an answer. Notice also from these examples that it is unlikely that components are universal features of language. We may, perhaps, assume that all societies distinguish between male and female and that thus (male) and (female) are universal components of language. Of course some languages may not make the distinction in the vocabulary, but it could then be said that the list of universal components was potential, i.e. available for all languages if not actually used. But the *come, go, bring, take* examples show that components are not related to simple physical features such as sex, and it becomes less plausible to assume that they are universal.

A particular characteristic of componential analysis is that it attempts as far as possible to treat components in terms of 'binary' opposites, e.g. between (male) and (female), (animate) and (inanimate), (adult) and (non adult). In this it clearly gives emphasis to the relation of complementarity (4.5). Notationally there is an advantage in such binary terms in that we can choose one only as the label and distinguish this in terms of plusses and minuses. Thus (male) and (female) are written as (+male) and (−male) and so on. We can, moreover, refer to the lack of a sex distinction as 'plus or minus' with the symbol (±male). But this works well only where there is a clear distinction; often there is indeterminacy, as with *tar* and *porridge* in relation to (solid)/(liquid).

In practice componential analysis has not been used simply in order to restate the relations discussed in earlier sections. Rather it has been used to bring out the logical relations that are associated with them. Thus by marking *man* as (+male) and *pregnant* as (−male), we can rule out **pregnant man.* Similarly by marking *boy* as (+male) (−adult) (+human) and *child* as (−adult) and (+human), we can establish that *There were two boys* entails *There were two children* and *Children are a nuisance* entails *Boys are a nuisance* (though the rules of entailment are obviously fairly complex).

Yet componential analysis does not handle all semantic relations well. First, it is difficult to reduce the relational opposites to components. For the relation of *parent/child* cannot simply be handled by assigning components to each, unless those components are in some sense directional. We could, that is to say, treat these as having the same components, but in a different 'direction', but by introducing 'direction' into components we are, in effect, admitting that they ARE relational and not simply 'atomic' components of meaning. Secondly, the componential analysis cannot remove the hierarchical characteristic of hyponymy. For the distinction (+male)/(−male) applies only to living (animate) things. Distinction in terms of these components, e.g. between *ram* and *ewe*, will hold only for items that are also marked as (+animate). In a straight hierarchical diagram this is easily shown, and is a natural consequence of the hierarchy. In a componential analysis it still has to be stated, for it is necessary to rule out not only *pregnant ram* but also *pregnant table*; the point here is that the component (female) is restricted to those items which also have (+animate). Componential analysis therefore has to state that, only if something is animate, may it be male or female with a formula such as +animate ±male. Again it will be obvious that such rules (called 'redundancy rules') are simply a disguised way of stating the hierarchical nature of the semantic distinctions.

Componential analysis can thus handle all the relations we have discussed, simply because it can be made to do so, with the relevant modifications. But it is doubtful whether it makes them clearer; it seems rather to obscure their differences.

The componential approach to semantics is basic to Katz and Fodor's 'The structure of a semantic theory'. This work has been of such interest that it deserves some consideration here and, although Katz has explicitly modified his views, I shall use it as the basis of the discussion.

As we have already seen (2.3), they are concerned essentially with ambiguity, anomaly and paraphrase. The arguments are, however, very largely based upon ambiguity – upon showing that a sentence may have two readings. Thus *The bill is large* is ambiguous until it is disambiguated by . . . *but need not be paid*.

Turning to the structure of vocabulary, they point out that a dictionary would distinguish between four meanings of the word *bachelor* – (i) a man who has never married, (ii) a young knight serving under the banner of another, (iii) someone with a first degree, (iv) a young male unmated fur seal during the mating season. These four meanings can, moreover, be partly differentiated by what they call 'markers' which are shown in round brackets, e.g. (human) (animal) and (male), together with some specific characteristics which are called 'distinguishers' and placed in square brackets, e.g. [first degree] in the case of the academic. The semantics of *bachelor* can thus be set out in a tree diagram:

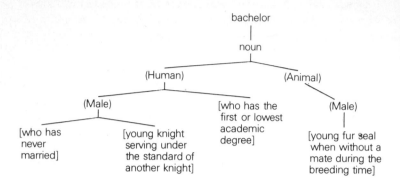

An important question, however, is 'How do we establish which precisely are the markers?' The answer that is given is that they are those features that allow us to disambiguate a sentence. An illustration provided by the authors is *The old bachelor finally died.* This cannot refer to the fur seal, because such bachelors are by definition young. It follows from this that (young) must be a marker for the fur seal, and that it must now appear not among the distinguishers as in the diagram, but as a marker.

The theory has one major drawback. There is, in theory, no limit to the number of markers that can be established. For (as we saw earlier in 3.1) any piece of information can be used to disambiguate and can thus function as a marker. For instance, *The bachelor wagged his flippers* is hardly ambiguous – it must refer to the fur seal. *The bachelor got his hair wet*, on the other hand, cannot refer to the fur seal, though it might refer to any of the other three. If we use the disambiguation test we have, for the fur seal, the markers (having flippers) and (not having hair) – and the list is endless. Katz later dropped the distinction between marker and distinguisher, but the difficulty remains. However we tackle the problem, we shall be faced with an infinite set of components, because in principle ANY piece of information may be used to disambiguate a sentence.

Componential analysis appears, at first sight, to be an attractive way of handling semantic relations. But it raises far too many difficulties to be at all workable.

5

LINGUISTIC CONTEXT

In Chapter 3 we discussed the possibility that meaning might be stated in terms of the occurrence of linguistic items within certain non-linguistic contexts. But it is also possible to argue that the meaning or at least part of the meaning of some elements, notably words, is stateable in terms of their LINGUISTIC context.

5.1 *Context as meaning*

The most extreme view, like the most extreme view of non-linguistic context, sees the meaning of the word as wholly stateable in terms of the context in which it occurred. Its origins lie in the view that linguistic analysis is largely concerned with the DISTRIBUTION of linguistic elements, a view associated most closely with the name of Zellig Harris. The notion of distribution was important to the so-called 'structuralist' school of linguistics that was at its height in the 1950s. It was believed that it was the task of the linguist to provide rigorous empirical methods for establishing and classifying his linguistic elements. Fundamental to this was the investigation of the environments in which they occur – their distribution. In phonology, for instance, we can establish that the two *l*'s of *leaf* and *feel* (which are very different phonetically) are the 'same' because they are in 'complementary' distribution – one occurs only in those environments that the other does not. By a similar argument the *-en* of *oxen* can be shown to be the 'same' as the *-s* of *cats* (purely in terms of distribution, without, that is to say, appealing to their meaning). On meaning, Harris commented, 'It may be presumed that any two morphemes having different meanings also differ in their distribution.' This is, perhaps, true enough, but we should usually argue that the difference in distribution was a result of the difference in meaning – *dog* is unlikely to occur in the same linguistic contexts as *apple*. But some linguists have suggested that the meaning of a word or morpheme is determined by the environment in which it occurs and that, for instance, two words can be considered synonymous if and only if they are totally interchangeable in all environments (even though this may mean there are no synonyms). M. Joos, indeed, specifically suggests that the linguist's meaning of a unit is 'the set of conditional probabilities' and he leaves 'outside' or 'practical' meaning to the sociologist.

This view deserves some consideration. It is not unlike the view that sees meaning in terms of the sense relations discussed in the last section, in that it deals with meaning in terms of relations between words, but this time with what we might call SYNTAGMATIC (as opposed to PARADIGMATIC) relations. By *syntagmatic* is meant the relationship that a linguistic element has with other elements in the stretch of language in which it occurs, while by *paradigmatic* is meant the relationship it has with elements with which it may be replaced or SUBSTITUTED. Thus if we consider *The cat is on the mat* we could talk of a syntagmatic relation between *cat* and *mat*, but if we compare this with *The dog is on the mat* we have a paradigmatic relation between *cat* and *dog*. Distribution, therefore, would deal with purely linguistic relations of a syntagmatic kind. Statement of meaning in terms of distribution has the same kind of attraction as statement of meaning in terms of sense in that both deal with observable features of language – with intra-linguistic relations, instead of the more nebulous association of language with the non-linguistic world of experience.

However, the attempt to state meaning in this way is not satisfactory. First, it does not deal with what is usually meant by *meaning*; in this respect it is even less satisfactory than the sense relations of the last chapter. It does not, in this way, meet what Lyons calls 'material adequacy' – the requirement that the linguist must cover, at least in part, the generally accepted scope of this term. Secondly, it is difficult to see how such an approach could do more than indicate sameness and difference of meaning (in terms of sameness and difference of distribution). It is not at all clear how it could say what meaning is, except by listing all the environments in which an element occurs. Moreover, we could equally state 'meaning' for phonemes (the sounds of a language), e.g. /f/ as in *feet*, *fly*, etc., for these, too, have stateable environments and would thus seem no less to have meaning. Yet it is normally agreed that phonemes do not have meaning. Thirdly, sameness and difference of meaning are not related to sameness and difference of distribution, for, in particular, antonyms, words with opposite meanings, will usually be found with almost identical distribution – both *wide* and *narrow*, for instance, with *road*, *hem*, *trouser-leg*, *band*, etc., whereas what seem to be synonyms often have quite different distribution. Fourthly, and most importantly, it is surely obvious that to define meaning in terms of distribution is very largely to put the cart before the horse. Words have different distribution BECAUSE they have different meanings.

5.2 *Collocation*

A much less extreme view is that of Firth who argued that 'You shall know a word by the company it keeps'. His familiar example was that of *ass* which occurred (in a now defunct variety of English) in *You silly* —, *Don't be such an* — and with a limited set of adjectives such as *silly, obstinate, stupid, awful* and (occasionally!) *egregious*. But for Firth this keeping company, which he called COLLOCATION, was merely PART of the meaning of a word. As we have seen, meaning was also to be found in the context of situation and all the other levels of analysis as well. Moreover, he was concerned not with total distribution, but with the more obvious and more interesting co-occurrences, the 'mutual expectancy of words', as he put it. We may see here that his collocation differed from the distributional analysis of Harris and others in much the same way as his context of situation differed from the behaviourist approaches. For Firth was concerned only with selecting those characteristics of the linguistic or non-linguistic context that he considered relevant, not with the totality of such contexts. The study of linguistic context is of interest to semantics for two reasons.

First, by looking at the linguistic contexts of words we can often distinguish between different meanings. Nida, for instance, discussed the use of *chair* in:

(1) *sat in a chair*
(2) *the baby's high chair*
(3) *the chair of philosophy*
(4) *has accepted a University chair*
(5) *the chairman of the meeting*
(6) *will chair the meeting*
(7) *the electric chair*
(8) *condemned to the chair*

These are clearly in pairs, giving four different meanings of the word. But this does not so much establish, as illustrate, differences of meaning. Dictionaries, especially the larger ones, quite rightly make considerable use of this kind of contextualisation.

Secondly, although in general the distribution of words may seem to be determined by their meaning (rather than vice versa) in some cases, this is not entirely true. We have already briefly noted (4.1) that *rancid* occurs with *bacon* and *butter*, and *addled* with *brains* and *eggs*, in spite of the fact that English has the terms *rotten* and *bad* and that *milk* is never *rancid* but only *sour*. We shall see (6.2) that *pretty child* and *buxom neighbour* would normally refer to females; here it is relevant to point out that we should not normally say *pretty boy* or *buxom man*, though *pretty girl* and *buxom woman* are quite normal. This characteristic of language is found in an extreme form in the collective words – *flock of sheep*, *herd of cows*, *school of whales*, *pride of lions*, and the rather more absurd examples such as *chattering of magpies, exaltation of larks.*

It is also the case that words may have more specific meanings in particular collocations. Thus we can speak of *abnormal* or *exceptional weather* if we have a heat wave in November, but *an exceptional child* is not an *abnormal child, exceptional* being used for greater than usual ability and *abnormal* to relate to some kind of defect (though, oddly, for 'euphemistic' reasons, *exceptional* is now being used by some people, especially in America, in place of *abnormal*).

It would, however, be a mistake to attempt to draw a clear distinguishing line between those collocations that are predictable from the meanings of the words that co-occur and those that are not (though some linguists have wished to restrict the term *collocation* to the latter). There have been some extensive investigations of collocation within texts and the results suggest that the co-occurrences are determined both by the meaning of the individual words and (though to a much lesser extent) by conventions about 'the company they keep'. For this reason, we cannot restrict the term in any precise way, though this does not necessarily preclude us from following Firth and investigating only those collocations that we feel to be interesting.

In spite of what has been said, it has been argued that ALL collocations are determined by the meaning of the words, though this point of view seems rather perverse. Thus it might be said that *pretty* means *handsome* in a female (or feminine) way, and that for this reason we can say *a pretty child* to mean 'a pretty girl' and not 'a handsome boy'. This is a little implausible and it is even less plausible to say that *rancid* means rotten in a butter-like or bacon-like way or that *addled* means rotten in the way that brains or eggs can be. For there are no obvious qualities of being rancid or addled that distinguish them from any other kind of rottenness. To say 'rotten (of butter)', 'rotten (of eggs)' is not then establishing a specific meaning for *rancid* or *addled*; it is merely indicating that there are the words to refer to rottenness when used with *butter* and *eggs.* The same point is even more obvious with the collective words. There is no meaning distinction between *herd* and *flock*, except that one is used with *cows* and the other with *sheep.*

Part of the difficulty arises from the fact that a word will often collocate with a number of other words that have something in common semantically. More strikingly (for negative examples often make the point more clearly), we find that individual words or sequences of words will NOT collocate with certain groups of words. Thus, though we may say *The rhododendron died,* we shall not say *The rhododendron passed away,* in spite of the fact that *pass away* seems to mean 'die'. But equally, of course, we should not use *pass away* with the names of any shrubs, not even with a shrub whose name we had heard for the first time. It is not very plausible to say that *pass away* indicates a special kind of dying that is not characteristic of shrubs. It is rather that there is a restriction on its use with a group of words that are semantically related. The restrictions are, it has been suggested (by A. McIntosh), a matter of RANGE – we know roughly the kind of nouns (in terms of their meaning) with which a verb or adjective may be used. So we do not reject specific collocations simply because we have never heard them before – we rely on our knowledge of the range.

We can, perhaps, see three kinds of collocational restriction. First, some are based wholly on the meaning of the item as in the unlikely *green cow.* Secondly, some are based on range – a word may be used with a whole set of words that have some semantic features in common. This accounts for the unlikeliness of *The rhododendron passed away* and equally of *the pretty boy* (*pretty* being used with words denoting females). Thirdly, some restrictions are collocational in the strictest sense, involving neither meaning nor range, as *addled* with *eggs* and *brains.* There may, of course, be borderline cases. It might be thought that *rancid* may be used with animal products of a certain type – perhaps *butter* and *bacon* have something in common. But why not *rancid cheese* or *rancid milk?*

5.3 *Idioms*

Idioms involve collocation of a special kind. Consider, for instance, *kick the bucket, fly off the handle, spill the beans, red herring*. For here we not only have the collocation of *kick* and *the bucket*, but also the fact that the meaning of the resultant combination is opaque (2.5) – it is not related to the meaning of the individual words, but is sometimes (though not always) nearer to the meaning of a single word (thus *kick the bucket* equals *die*).

Even where an idiom is semantically like a single word it does not function like one. Thus we will not have a past tense **kick-the-bucketed*. Instead, it functions to some degree as a normal sequence of grammatical words, so that the past tense form is *kicked the bucket*. But there are a great number of grammatical restrictions. A large number of idioms contain a verb and a noun, but although the verb may be placed in the past tense, the number of the noun can never be changed. We have *spilled the beans*, but not **spill the bean* and equally there is no **fly off the handles*, **kick the buckets*, **put on good faces*, **blow one's tops*, etc. Similarly, with *red herring* the noun may be plural, but the adjective cannot be comparative (the *-er* form). Thus we find *red herrings* but not **redder herring*.

There are also plenty of syntactic restrictions. Some idioms have passives, but others do not. *The law was laid down* and *The beans have been spilled* are all right (though some may question the latter), but **The bucket was kicked* is not. But in no case could we say *It was the —* (*beans that were spilled, law that was laid down, bucket that was kicked*, etc.). The restrictions vary from idiom to idiom. Some are more restricted or 'frozen' than others.

A very common type of idiom in English is what is usually called the 'phrasal verb', the combination of verb plus adverb of the kind *make up, give in, put down*. The meaning of these combinations cannot be predicted from the individual verb and adverb and in many cases there is a single verb with the same or a very close meaning — *invent, yield, quell*. Not all combinations of this kind are idiomatic, of course. *Put down* has a literal sense too and there are many others that are both idiomatic and not, e.g. *take in* as in *The conjuror took the audience in, The woman took the homeless children in.* There are even degrees of idiomaticity since one can *make up* a story, *make up* a fire or *make up* one's face. Moreover, it is not only sequences of verb plus adverb that may be idiomatic. There are also sequences of verb plus preposition, such as *look after* and *go for,* and sequences of verb, adverb and preposition, such as *put up with* ('tolerate') or *do away with* ('kill').

There are also what we may call partial idioms, where one of the words has its usual meaning, the other has a meaning that is peculiar to the particular sequence. Thus *red hair* refers to hair, but not hair that is red in strict colour terms. Comedians have fun with partial idioms of this kind, e.g. when instructed to *make a bed* they bring out a set of carpenter's tools. An interesting set involves the word *white,* for white coffee is brown in colour, white wine is usually yellow, and white people are pink. Yet *white* is, perhaps, idiomatic only to some degree – it could be interpreted 'the lightest in colour of that usually to be found'. Not surprisingly *black* is used as its antonym for coffee and people (though again neither are black in colour terms), yet it is not used for wine. Thus it can be seen that even partial idiomaticity can be a matter of degree and may in some cases be little more than a matter of collocational restriction. On a more comic level there is partial idiomaticity in *raining cats and dogs* (in Welsh it rains *old women and sticks*!).

What is and what is not an idiom is, then, often a matter of degree. It is very difficult, moreover, to decide whether a word or a sequence of words is opaque. We could, perhaps, define idioms in terms of non-equivalence in other languages, so that *kick the bucket, red herring,* etc., are idioms because they cannot be directly translated into French or German. But this will not really work. The French for nurse is *garde-malade,* but while this cannot be directly translated into English it is quite transparent, obviously meaning someone who looks after the sick. On the other hand, *look after* seems quite idiomatic, yet it can be quite directly translated into Welsh (*edrych ar ôl*).

5.4 *Collocation and grammar*

Firth saw collocation as just one of his levels or statements of meaning. Others have attempted to integrate it more closely to the other levels of linguistic analysis, to argue, for instance, that it may be handled within the level of lexis, which is related in a fairly direct and, in theory, precise way to grammar.

There is one attempt to handle collocation WITHIN the grammar (or 'syntax'), as distinct from the phonology and semantics. This is in Chomsky's *Aspects of the theory of syntax*. Chomsky is concerned with a grammar that, given a set of appropriate rules, will generate all and only the grammatical sentences of a language. What is relevant to semantics is that he is concerned with restrictions on the co-occurrence of items within a sentence, so that we shall not permit *The idea cut the tree, I drank the bread, He frightened that he was coming, He elapsed the man.* In all these examples it is clear that we have chosen items that, in some way, do not 'fit' the verbs. The last examples are clearly a matter of grammar in that *frightened* does not take a *that*-clause, while *elapse* is an intransitive verb that does not take any object at all. With the other two examples it is a matter, however, of the incompatibility of lexical items of certain nouns (as subjects or objects) with certain verbs. While noting the difference between these two types, Chomsky proposes to deal with them in similar ways. In both cases he states, as part of the specification of the verb, the environment in which it may occur. Thus *elapse* is shown as not occurring with an object noun phrase, and *frighten* not occurring with a following *that*-clause (or rather it is NOT shown that they can so occur, since the specification will state what is possible, not what is not possible). Similarly *cut* will be shown to need a 'concrete' subject, and *drink* a 'liquid' object. This is achieved in terms of components, by stating that the relevant subject and object must have the components (concrete) and (liquid). These are SELECTIONAL RESTRICTIONS. Any sentence which does not comply to them is ruled out and the grammar will not generate it (see also 7.1).

Although this appears very neat it is quite unsatisfactory for a number of reasons. First, we have, once again, the problem of the limitless number of components required (see 4.7 and also 6.2). For if we are to rule out all the anomalous sentences, we shall have to include all relevant information – and this is infinite. Secondly, the theory fails to make a distinction between what is grammatical and what is lexical; this we shall discuss in more detail in 7.1. Thirdly, it cannot account, without considerable complications, for the many occasions in which such selectional restrictions are legitimately broken. This is possible with verbs of saying, thinking, etc. as in *John thought we could drink bread*, or with some negatives, e.g. *You can't drink bread*. It is obvious that we are concerned here with 'making sense', and that is a matter of semantics rather than grammar. For we can be grammatical and still not make sense as Chomsky himself illustrated with his famous *Colourless green ideas sleep furiously*. It is a mistake, then, to attempt to handle these essentially semantic relations between lexical items within the grammar of a language (though it is by no means certain that they can be handled in any complete and consistent way in ANY part of the linguistic analysis).

Finally, we may notice that quite different grammatical constructions seem to retain what are the same collocational restrictions within them. Thus we find alongside *a strong argument, the strength of the argument, he argued strongly, his argument was strengthened* (Halliday 1966). The collocation does not hold simply, that is to say, between *strong* and *argument* but between all the related words *strong, strength, strongly, strengthen* and *argue, argument*. It follows that if collocational restrictions are to be handled in the lexicon, the basic lexical item will have to be not the words (lexemes) *strong, strengthen,* etc., but some more general item that subsumes them all. Firth referred to groups of related words as the 'formal scatter'. It is with collocations between scatters, not words, that we should be concerned.

6

MEANING AND THE SENTENCE

In much of the previous discussion it has been assumed that we were talking about the meaning of words, though it is also clear that we must allow sentences to have meaning too. In this chapter we will consider the analysis of the meaning of sentences and, in particular, how it can be related to the meaning of words.

6.1 *Word and sentence*

It is clear, to begin with, that sentences and words do not have meaning in the same way. If we consider meaning in terms of reference in the wide sense of the term, i.e. as saying something about the world about us, it is reasonable to believe that only sentences can have meaning. In so far as words have referential meaning, they acquire it either through being parts of sentences or, more specifically, through ostensive definitions (2.3), but even ostensive definitions are achieved only by means of sentences of the kind *This is a* . . . Referential meaning, then, seems to be a characteristic of sentences. Meaning in terms of sense, on the other hand, appears, at least in part, to belong largely to words. We have already seen some examples – *ram/ewe, father/son, wide/narrow, male/female*, etc. Dictionaries are, of course, very largely concerned with words, and thus with sense relations (but see 2.5).

Admittedly utterances sometimes consist of single words. It is simple enough to imagine a situation in which someone may simply say *Horses*. But even in such cases it is reasonable to treat these utterances as sentences, but as incomplete one-word sentences (some grammarians refer to them as 'minor' sentences). Treating them as incomplete is justified by the fact that, given the context, they always can be completed. Thus *Horses* may be a reply to *What are those animals?* and thus seen as an incomplete version of *They are horses*. We can thus define sentences in such a way as to make it possible for them to consist, in certain circumstances, of single words. There is no equivocation in talking about one-word sentences – the essential point is that conversations do not normally simply consist of words, except when such words are formed into sentences, and it is in this sense that sentences, but not words, may be said to be meaningful.

If we establish a distinction between sentence meaning and word meaning, a major problem will be that of relating the two. Some scholars believe that the meaning of a sentence can be derived from the sum of the word meanings, and we shall discuss sentence meaning in these terms in the next section. Yet anyone who considers reference to be important may plausibly argue that this is back-to-front, that, since only sentences have referential meaning, the meaning of words is derived from the meaning of the sentences in which they occur and not vice versa.

6.2 *Projection rules*

We have already discussed componential analysis, and in particular the use made of it by Katz and Fodor to characterise anomalous and ambiguous sentences (4.7) as well as its function in Chomsky's selectional restrictions (5.4). In this section I shall attempt to explain briefly the way in which it is envisaged that the theory may take us from the meaning of words to the meaning of sentences.

In simple language what they propose is a set of rules to combine the meanings of individual lexical items. The rules are called PROJECTION RULES, the combination is referred to as AMALGAMATION, and the meanings are called PATHS. The paths are no more than the structural analysis of the meaning as shown in diagram form in 4.3 – and the amalgamation is thus a combination of the markers and distinguishers. Projection rules are needed since it is necessary to state what may be amalga-

mated with what, and in what order. This will be determined
by the grammatical status of the elements – we shall combine
adjective with noun, noun phrase with verb, and so on.

The example chosen by Katz and Fodor as an illustration
of the application of the projection rules is *The man hit the
colorful ball* (since I use their example, I will retain the American spelling). We must first establish the grammatical status
of the lexical items, that *colorful* is an adjective and *ball* a
noun and that together with *the* they form a noun phrase, and
so on, but we need not bother with the details here. We then
have to amalgamate the paths of the various lexical items. We
begin with *colorful* and *ball*. In one path for *colorful* we find
a marker (color) referring to actual colour, but there is another
path in which the marker is (evaluative) to deal with the meaning of *colorful* to refer to the 'colorful' nature of any aesthetic
object. *Ball* has three paths, one with the marker (Social
activity), the other two with the marker (Physical object) but
distinguished by the distinguishers [Having globular shape] and
[Solid missile for projection by engine of war]. We are concerned, that is to say, with the ball at which people dance, the
'ordinary' round ball and cannon balls. (There is much more
information not relevant for our purpose.) But there is a further and vital piece of information; the first *colorful* is specified
as occurring in the environment of either (Physical object) or
(Social activity), the second in the environment of either
(Aesthetic object) – this is, in fact, irrelevant for us – or (Social
activity). Although we have three paths for *ball* and two for
colorful, when we amalgamate their paths to produce *colorful
ball* we shall not have six (three times two) amalgamated paths,
but only four. The reason is, of course, that the second path of
colorful (evaluative) will not amalgamate with that of *ball* with
the marker (Physical object). In general terms we are saying
that all three balls can be colourful in the literal sense of having
colour, but only the ball at which people dance can be colourful in the evaluative sense – the other two balls cannot. (I am
not concerned with the factual accuracy of these statements,
only with them as examples.)

We now amalgamate *colorful ball* with *hit*. *Hit* has two paths, one indicating collision, the other indicating striking, and both occur in the environment (Physical object). We shall not, however, now have eight (two times four) derived paths, since neither will amalgamate with *colorful ball* with the marker (Social activity), since in neither sense of *hit* can this kind of ball be hit. We shall instead have only four possibilities. Finally, we can amalgamate the path of *The man* (one path only), and so eventually derive four readings only for the sentence (colliding with or striking either an ordinary ball or a cannon ball).

In our previous discussion (4.7 and 5.4) we saw roughly how componential analysis has been used to deal with anomalies and selectional restrictions. More precisely, projection rules handle such sentences as *★The idea cut the tree* or *★John drank the bread* by assigning them no readings at all. Just as some of the amalgamated paths are ruled out for *The man hit the colorful ball*, so all paths are ruled out for these anomalous sentences and no readings result. Indeed, an anomalous sentence is to be DEFINED as one that has no readings. We have seen some of the problems with componential analysis in general and with its use in dealing with selectional restrictions. But there are further difficulties in the attempt to use it to move from word to sentence.

First, if we merely add components together as we use the projection rules then it will follow that *Cats chase mice* and *Mice chase cats* have exactly the same meaning. The point is clear – *chase* is essentially relational, just as are the relational opposites of 4.6. Indeed the active/passive relationship is essentially one of relational opposites since *Cats chase mice* entails *Mice are chased by cats*. The 'direction' of the relation is important and has to be stated. As we saw in 4.7 it is possible to 'insert' direction into components, but that is essentially to treat them not as components, but as relations.

Secondly, a problem arises in that the same component may at times merely provide the environment for amalgamation, at others be part of the derived path (i.e. part of the meaning of the resultant combination). Consider the word *pregnant*. If we follow the procedure for *colorful ball* we shall wish to say that this will occur only in the environment of (−male) so as to permit *pregnant woman*, but not *pregnant man*. But we can also say *pregnant horse*, though *horse* (unlike *mare*) is not marked (−male) and, moreover, *pregnant horse* clearly refers to a female creature and can be combined with . . . *gave birth*. In such an example the (−male) component has come from the adjective not the noun, yet the rules will have made no provision for this (nor can they very easily if, in general, we wish to treat *pregnant* as compatible only with female nouns). There are many other similar examples – *pretty child, buxom neighbour*, where the noun phrase is presumably (−male) but the nouns *child* and *neighbour* are not. Of course, ways can be found to deal with a problem such as this; one way (suggested by U. Weinreich) is to talk about a special 'transference rule' which 'transfers' the relevant component. But such examples show that componential analysis does not provide a simple way of proceeding from the meaning of lexical items to the meaning of sentences by a process of the adding together of the components through amalgamation.

6.3 *Predicate calculus*

We have already noted that in a sentence the verb is often best seen as a relational feature and, indeed, that active and passive sentences could be handled as if they were relational opposites (4.6). Analysis in relational terms seems to offer a far more satisfactory solution to the problem of sentence meaning than componential analysis. In essence such analysis will have much in common with the predicate calculus used by logicians. But the logicians' use of this is concerned almost entirely with the statement of logical relations between sentences rather than with the means of stating the meaning of sentences for its own sake, and I shall not, therefore, attempt to explain PREDICATE CALCULUS in logicians' terms, but rather to follow proposals made by Bierwisch, though I shall not follow his notations throughout or use his examples.

The meaning of a sentence is a PROPOSITION (it will be obvious that we are to deal only with propositional or cognitive meaning and we must agree to ignore the difficulties raised in Chapter 2). Propositions consist of TERMS, which are of two types, PREDICATES and ARGUMENTS. The predicates are the relational terms and usually correspond to verbs in sentences; the arguments are the terms that are related, and usually correspond to nouns. For example in *John loves Mary* we have a relation (a predicate) expressed in *loves* and two items (two arguments) expressed in *John* and *Mary*. If we write the predicate in square brackets (logicians use round brackets, but I shall need these for another purpose and so shall, with Bierwisch, use square brackets) we arrive at the formula [Love] John, Mary. One important but obvious point is that the arguments are ORDERED in that [Love] Mary, John will be the formula for something different – *Mary loves John*. Thus using x and y as VARIABLES we can say that [Love] x, y is distinct from [Love] y, x. It is, of course, true, as we saw in 4.6, that SOME relations are symmetrical. An example is provided by the English *be married to* since *John is married to Mary* entails *Mary is married to John*. We find, then, that we have to say that [Married to] x, y entails [Married to] y, x but this is a property of this particular predicate (and a few others), and not one of predicates in general.

A major advantage of this approach is that it can handle 'atomic' components as well as relational ones. For we may regard such components as a relation involving just one argument. Let us take as an example *Bill is Harry's father*. Here we want to express both the relationship of 'parent of' and the component (+male). We can symbolise [Parent] Bill, Harry. [Male] Bill (the full stop indicates 'and'), i.e. 'Bill is the parent of Harry' and 'Bill is male'.

This example shows that there may be one or two arguments. The distinction is usually made in terms of 'one-place' and 'two-place' predicates. There may be three-place predicates, predicates with three arguments. An example is *give* as in *John gave Bill a book*. For *give*, then, we have the formula [Give] x, y, z. There may also be four-, or five-place predicates and so on. In practice, however, these will not be needed. Indeed, it can be argued that all can be reduced to combinations of one-place and two-place predicates (see below).

Predicate calculus provides a simple method of dealing with what is known in grammar as SUBORDINATION, by allowing a proposition to function as an argument. Thus we may wish to analyse *Fred thinks that John loves Mary* by saying that the predicate [Think] has two arguments, *Fred* and the proposition *John loves Mary*. We need to indicate that the whole proposition [Love] John, Mary (*John loves Mary*) is one of the arguments of [Think] and must symbolise [Think] Fred, ([Love] John, Mary). (I use the round brackets for the obvious purpose of showing that, in relation to [Think], ([Love] John, Mary) is a single unit, one argument.) Thus a proposition with its own predicate and arguments can also be an argument of another 'higher' proposition.

There is, of course, more to it than this. We want also to be able to account for modifiers such as *brave* in *brave men*. But to do this we need some notion of 'who is', 'who are', 'which is', etc. Moreover, we want to distinguish between *The brave men* and *Brave men* or *The brave man* and *A brave man*. Logicians make a distinction between 'all' and 'some' with the operators $\forall$ (all) and $\exists$ ('there exists at least one'), but as linguists we probably need a different set of distinctions. We certainly need to distinguish between 'the' and 'a' in *the dog* and *a dog*. But *a dog* is ambiguous as can be seen in the sentence *I'm looking for a dog*. For we can continue either *and when I find it . . .* or *and when I find one . . . .* In the first case we are looking for a particular, specific dog, in the second for 'any' dog. Both are, of course, different from *I'm looking for the dog*. We should, then, modify the logician's analysis and postulate three operators Def ('definite'), Spec ('specific'), and Ind ('indefinite') to refer to *the dog*, *a dog* (a particular dog) and *a dog* (any dog) in the examples we have just been considering. These operators can be roughly translated as 'the entity such that . . .', 'a particular entity such that . . .' and 'any entity such that . . .'. We now symbolise 'the dog' as (Def x) ([Dog] x) i.e., 'The entity x such that x is a dog'. Similarly *a dog* will be either (Spec x) ([Dog] x) or (Ind x) ([Dog] x), depending on whether we mean a particular dog or not.

Let us now consider *the brave man*. The formula for this will be (Def x) ([Man] x. [Brave] x) – i.e., 'The entity x such that x is a man and x is brave'. Notice again the use of the round brackets – the whole of 'x is a man and x is brave' is part of the 'such that' qualification (or in more technical terminology is within the scope of (Def x)). We can now proceed to more complex items. For instance, the formula for *The brave man ran away* will be [Ran away] (Def x) ([Man] x. [Brave] x), i.e., 'The entity x such that x is a man and x is brave ran away'. For *The young boy loves the beautiful girl* we may propose [Love] (Def x) ([Boy] x. [Young] x), (Def y) ([Girl] y. [Beautiful] y). However, it must be stressed that this is a simplified account; there are many problems that arise that cannot be considered here. One such problem is that with the plural *The young boys love the beautiful girls* the formula, as given here, would mean that each boy loved each girl (the predicate relates every x with every y), yet this is not the natural interpretation of the English sentence which simply says there was a loving relationship between the two groups, but is otherwise quite vague.

In the examples we have considered so far the semantic interpretation has not been very different from that suggested by the syntax of the sentence. But it is possible to break propositions down into far more basic elements than those indicated by the actual words of the sentence. For instance, we might think of treating *Bill gave Harry a book* in terms of a three-place predicate [Give] – [Give] x, y, z. But we could, instead, interpret the sentence as 'Bill caused Harry to have a book'. The formula then becomes [Cause] x, ([Have] y, z) where the arguments of [Cause] are x ('Bill') and the proposition [Have] y, z ('Harry have a book'). Similarly we might treat *kill* as 'cause to be dead' or 'cause to be not alive'. The latter is more favoured, but it involves the use of another logical operator 'not' which is symbolised ∼. The formula for *John killed Mary* would then be [Cause] x, ([Become] y, ([∼ Alive] y)) i.e., 'John caused Mary become Mary not alive'; notice that both [Cause] and [Become] have a proposition as their second argument.

This kind of analysis is often written out in 'tree diagrams' which are used for syntax. Thus for our last example see the diagram below:

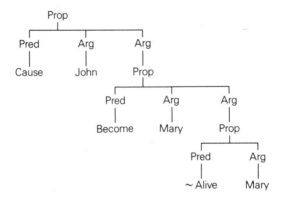

It is a mistake, however, to confuse such a semantic representation with the syntax of a sentence. In particular *John killed Mary* is not identical with *John caused Mary to become dead*, since it is (just) possible to say *On Thursday John caused Mary to become dead on Saturday* but not *On Thursday John killed Mary on Saturday*. The difference, of course, lies in the temporal marking of the predicates, and if there is only one verb in the original sentence there cannot be more than one time indication. We have not discussed tense and time, nor can we now do so, but clearly they (as well as all the semantics of place, manner, etc.) have eventually to be accounted for.

As a means of showing sentence meaning (if we can restrict meaning to propositional or cognitive meaning), some kind of predicate calculus seems to be the most satisfactory. It allows us to move from word to sentence in that the formula for each word will usually form part of the whole sentence formula – though it will often be more than a single predicate or argument – as we have seen for *give* and *kill*. But it is equally clear that it will be far more complex than has so far been suggested.

6.4 *Analytic and synthetic*

The arguments in much of this chapter and in Chapter 4 have assumed that we can isolate the logical relations that hold between words and, moreover, that these can and must be handled within a semantic theory. This, however, assumes that we can distinguish between two kinds of truth, the one NECESSARY and depending upon logical relations, the other CONTINGENT and depending upon facts about the world. The distinction is (or appears to be) clear enough in:

> *All bachelors are unmarried.*
> *All bachelors are miserable.*

The truth of the first of these is a logical one – it depends on the definition of the word *bachelor* and its relation to *unmarried*. This is an ANALYTIC truth, and the sentence is analytically true. The truth of the second (if, in fact, it is true!) depends wholly upon an observed fact about bachelors, and in no way results from the definition of the words involved. This is a SYNTHETIC truth, and the sentence is synthetically true.

It is clear enough that the sense relations of Chapter 4 related to analytic truth – it is involved in the antonymy (complementarity) relation of *male* and *female* and in all the hyponymy relations, since *This is scarlet* logically entails *This is red*. It also seems to be involved in all the relations that may be handled in a componential analysis. In actual fact Katz and Fodor do not establish (Unmarried) as a marker of bachelor, but it clearly must be one since 'unmarried' is part of the definition of *bachelor* (in one sense), and we can easily justify the presence of such a marker with the sentence *The bachelor was unhappy when his wife died*. This cannot refer to *bachelor* in the sense required (it would have to refer to a B.A., B.Sc., etc.) and we can thus assign the marker (Unmarried) to *bachelor* in order to disambiguate.

Unfortunately language is not as tidy as this might suggest, and it is by no means always clear whether a sentence is analytically or synthetically true. This is easily illustrated where the relevant class is not well defined. Consider:

> All carnivores eat meat.
> All mammals produce live young.

It might be thought that these are analytically true, that it is part of the definition of carnivore that it eats meat, that it is part of the definition of mammal that it produces live young. However, the giant panda, which is classified by zoologists as a carnivore, lives almost exclusively on bamboo shoots, while the platypus, which is classified as a mammal, lays eggs. In the light of this the sentences above are not analytically true, and are, moreover, synthetically false. Of course, we can re-define *carnivore* and *mammal* to exclude the panda and the platypus and retain the analytic truth. But whether we are involved in an analytic or a synthetic judgment depends on the definition of *carnivore* and *mammal*. The scientist is perfectly entitled to modify his definitions to ensure that they are watertight. If he comes across a new plant, or a creature that seems to invalidate his definitions, he can change them. For instance, the characteristic of meat-eating could well have been included in the original definition of carnivore, but dropped when the giant panda was found, since this creature has other characteristics of carnivores but does not eat meat. Thus by dropping the most 'obvious' characteristic the scientist would have been able to preserve the rest of his classificatory system.

The scientist, then, can decide to make his definitions in such a way that he knows whether a sentence is analytically or synthetically true. But ordinary speakers of a language cannot do this, for the definition of a word is not within the individual's power. We may, then be faced with problems of the kind 'When is a stool not a stool?' For I am not at all sure whether *This stool has a broken back* is anomalous (Is part of the definition of stool that it has no back?), or whether *All pies have pastry on top* is analytically true (Is part of the definition of *pie* that it has a top?). When we turn to sets of objects such as *chair, armchair, settee, couch, divan, chaise-longue,* etc., we shall find ourselves in numerous problems of this kind. I am not at all clear whether 'armchair without arms' is a contradiction in terms since the 'lady's chair' in a suite used to be larger than the rest (except the 'gentleman's chair'), but it had no arms. With verbs the problems are even more difficult. Can a man *trot* at fifteen miles an hour or take strides of eighteen inches? The answers are not at all certain, yet the decision whether a sentence is or is not anomalous will depend upon such answers.

In practice there is no difficulty. The problem of analytic/ synthetic does not prevent us from communicating or from writing dictionaries. But the fact that there are these problems should deter us from looking for answers of a purely logical kind. Indeed it is, or should be, clear that the study of semantics is not advanced by being 'reduced' to logic. Logical relations are not relations that in some mysterious way 'underlie' human language. They are merely a convenient way of restating in a precise formulaic way some of the semantic features of language. But their precision is not, as often assumed, always a virtue, since it disguises the complexities and difficulties.

7

SEMANTICS AND GRAMMAR

The meaning of grammatical elements has been ignored in previous chapters. Yet some books on semantics have devoted a great deal of space to the investigation of the meaning of what are essentially grammatical characteristics of language. There is obviously no place in a book such as this for a detailed semantic analysis of the grammatical categories of English or of other languages as well. (There is equally no place for a detailed discussion of the meaning of all the lexical items!). But there are three topics that seem worth discussing. The first concerns the status of grammar in relation to the lexicon and semantics. This with exemplification will occupy the first three sections. We shall then turn to some grammatical categories that appear to relate directly to the context of situation (7.4) and, finally, to some notions that have been thought to be relevant to the grammatical-cum-semantic structure of sentences (7.5).

7.1 *Grammar and lexicon*

We noted, in 2.5, the distinction made by Henry Sweet in terms of full words and form words. Full words are essentially those that can be dealt with satisfactorily in the dictionary, while the form words (although always listed in dictionaries) have to be discussed in the grammar of the language. For modern linguists the distinction is between LEXICON and grammar. Other scholars have made similar distinctions. An American linguist, C. C. Fries, recognised only four 'parts of speech' but fifteen sets of 'function words'. The parts of speech were, in effect, noun, verb, adjective and adverb, though Fries quite deliberately refused to call them by these traditional names; examples from each of the sets of function words are *the, may, not, very, and, at, do, there, why, although, oh, yes, listen!, please, let's*.

Grammar, however, is not restricted to the study of form or function words. It is concerned, more widely, with categories such as tense, gender, number and with syntactic functions such as subject and object. Some of these may be marked in a language by form words, but they may equally be marked by morphemes (assuming we accept the suggestions in 2.5) or even by the order of the words. While there is a problem of establishing what are the relevant grammatical categories in any language (see next section), it is irrelevant for semantics whether a grammatical category is indicated by a form word, a morpheme or the order of the words. For example, we find that English marks past tense with the past tense morpheme (usually indicated as *-ed*). But there is no similar morpheme to indicate the future; this is marked by the verbs *shall* and *will* or by *be going to* (it may also be indicated by other verbal forms with the appropriate adverbs as in *I'm flying to Cairo tomorrow* and *I fly to Cairo tomorrow*). Other languages may use inflection where English and most familiar languages use form words. Thus the English conjunctions *after, when, while, if* are translated into Bilin (a Cushitic language of Ethiopia), by endings of the verb. Nearer home, Finnish has a very complex 'case' system, containing not only 'nominative', 'accusative', 'ablative' etc., all of which are familiar from Latin, but also 'elative', 'illative', 'adessive', 'essive' and others. These last ones would translate English *out of, into, on, as*.

In modern linguistics the problem of the distinction between the grammar and the lexicon is often posed in terms of the distinction between sentences that are unacceptable or 'deviant' for grammatical reasons, and those that are excluded on lexical grounds. There is no apparent difficulty about recognising a grammatically deviant sentence. An example would be **The boys is in the garden*. This breaks only one grammatical rule, but we can easily invent sentences that seem to conform to no rules at all as **Been a when I tomato*. In contrast we shall rule out on different grounds *The water is fragile*, *The flower walked away*. With these the issue is one of collocational possibilities or selectional restrictions (see 5.2, 5.4), which determine the co-occurrence of lexical items and here rule out the co-occurrence of *water* with *fragile* and *flower* with *walk*.

There have, however, been opposing views on the question whether these two kinds of restriction, one grammatical, the other lexical, are, in principle, different. One argument to sustain the difference is that a sentence can be grammatically correct, yet at the same time totally deviant in lexical terms. Thus Chomsky invented the sentence *Colourless green ideas sleep furiously*, which seems impeccable grammatically, yet is lexically completely unacceptable. If a sentence can thus conform to grammar, but be completely deviant lexically, it would seem that grammar and lexicon are distinct. Earlier, incidentally, Carnap had made the same point by inventing a sentence that does not contain any English word at all yet seems to be quite grammatical in terms of English – *Pirots carulize elatically*.

In spite of this, Chomsky later attempted to handle selectional restrictions as part of the grammar, as was noted in 5.4 *Colourless green ideas sleep furiously* would now be ungrammatical. We there saw some of the difficulties that this raises, but the important question is not whether it is possible to handle such restrictions as part of the grammar, but rather whether there is any justification at all for doing so. For we surely do not wish to say that *John drank the meat* is ungrammatical in the same sense as is *The boys is in the garden*. The difference seems clear enough to us as native speakers of the language, for, if we are confronted with deviant sentences of these two types, our reactions are different. If a grammatical rule is broken, we can, and usually will, correct the sentence, e.g. to *The boys are in the garden*, while if the sentence conforms to no grammatical rules we simply rule it out as gibberish. Where, however, the deviance lies in the collocational (selectional) restrictions, i.e. is lexical, we shall usually try to 'make sense' of the sentence by looking for a context in which it might be used. For instance, *John drinks fish* might seem to be deviant, until we think about fish soup, and it is by no means difficult to find a poetic interpretation (or even possibly a scientific one) for *The water is fragile*. Even Chomsky's *Colourless green ideas sleep furiously* can be (and has been) given an interpretation, far fetched though it has to be.

The lexical restrictions, it has been suggested (by W. Haas), are not a matter of rules but of tendencies, not of Yes/no, but of More/less, when judged in terms of deviance. Unfortunately this leads us to the problem 'When is a rule a rule?', for there is no clear line between grammatical and lexical deviance. Some sentences are clearly ungrammatical and are simply to be ruled out or corrected, while others are odd only in a lexical way and can, with some imagination, be contextualised. But there are others that are half-way, and we are not really sure whether their deviance is lexical or grammatical.

Consider, for example, **The dog scattered*. This is not simply a matter of the collocation of *dog* with *scatter*, for the verb *scatter* is normally used only with plural nouns (*The dogs scattered*), or with collective nouns (*The herd scattered*). It would seem, therefore, that a grammatical rule is being broken and that we should emend to *The dogs scattered* (or *The dog was scattered*). But cannot we imagine a dog with magical powers whose way of avoiding its enemies was to break into many pieces and 'scatter' over a wide area? Indeed we can, and so we have found a possible, if far fetched, contextualisation for *The dog scattered*. The deviance would seem, therefore, to be lexical rather than grammatical. But I am not really sure. Can we say *The dog scattered* even in such a context? Or would *The dog scattered itself* be more appropriate? My indecision here shows that we are on the borderline of grammar and lexicon.

I said earlier that in attempting to contextualise a possibly deviant sense we try to 'make sense' of it. The question whether the collocations are possible is often, that is to say, a matter of meaning. The next section concerns grammar and meaning and some of the examples quoted in the last part of it will be making what is essentially the same point.

7.2 *Formal grammar*

Most of the traditional grammarians assumed that grammatical categories were essentially semantic. Nouns were defined as names of things, gender was concerned with sex, while plural simply meant 'more than one'.

On the other hand, many linguists have argued that grammar must be kept distinct from semantics and that grammatical categories must be wholly defined in terms of the FORM of the language, the actually observable features. (It is unfortunate that the term *form* is also used for *form* words as opposed to *full* words. This is a completely different and much more restricted use of the term and must not be confused with its use here.) One of the earliest statements is in Sapir, but Sapir, it will be remembered, believed in linguistic relativity (3.4), and his point was essentially that, since each language had a different formal structure, it presented a different world. Bloomfield took a similar line for a different reason (3.3) – that we must be 'scientific' and that the study of meaning was a weak point in linguistic theory. He insisted, therefore, that formal features, not meaning, should be the starting point of a linguistic discussion.

There are two good arguments for excluding meaning from grammar, i.e. in favour of FORMAL GRAMMAR. The first is that meaning is often very vague and meaning categories are not easily delineated. Moreover, because of this vagueness, what might seem to be obvious semantic categories are often in fact definable only in terms of the formal features of a language (to this extent Whorf may have been right). If, then, the grammatical categories are given semantic definitions, the definitions are circular. An excellent example is the definition so often found in grammar books of a noun as 'a word used for naming anything'. The difficulty is that we have no way of establishing what 'anything' may be. To be of any value the definition must establish independently of the language what are 'the things' that may be named. We find that in English such things include fire, speed, place, intelligence, suffering, as well as objects such as tables and chairs. Moreover, it includes 'redness' and 'blackness', but not 'red' and 'black'. What reason have we for believing that these are all 'things' and how, in particular, do we know that *redness* and *blackness* are names of 'things', while *red* and *black* are not? Similarly, why does *rain* refer to a 'thing', while *It's raining* does not? It is reported that there are some languages in which words for 'river', 'spring', etc., are essentially verbs so that a literal translation would be 'It's rivering' rather than 'There's a river' (see 3.4). How, then, do we recognise 'things?' The answer is painfully simple – 'things' are what are designated by nouns. The definition of the noun in terms of 'naming anything' is thus completely circular; the circularity arises because we have no non-linguistic way of defining 'things'.

A second argument for formal grammar is that, even when we can establish semantic and grammatical categories independently, they often do not coincide. One of the most famous (or infamous) examples is found in the comparison of grammatical number, singular and plural, with numerical quantity; examples are *wheat* and *oats*. That these are singular and plural respectively is shown not so much by the -*s* ending of *oats* as by the agreement with the verb – *The wheat is in the barn, The oats are in the barn.* Yet in terms of 'one' and 'more than one' *wheat* and *oats* cannot be distinguished. No one, surely, would seriously argue that *wheat* is a single mass, while *oats* consist of a collection of individual grains. There are many other similar examples. *Hair* is singular in English, but French and Italian have a plural noun, *cheveux, capelli*; it is not to be supposed that there is any difference in the way we look at hair. Similarly gender and sex are distinct in German and French. The German words for 'young woman' are neuter, *Mädchen* and *Fräulein*, while the feminine *la sentinelle* in French may refer to a strapping young male. In English tense is not directly

related to time since the past tense is used for future time in
e.g. *If he came tomorrow* . . . (see 3.4).

It is clear from such examples that the basic grammatical
categories of a language must be established independently of
their meaning. From this it follows that there may well be
different systems in different languages; that there are is a
fact that is well known to all students of language.

Nevertheless once we have established the formal categories,
we can proceed to discuss their meaning (as we shall be doing in
the next three sections). We shall then find that there is some
correlation between e.g. gender and sex, tense and time, grammatical number and enumeration, though the correlation will
never be exact. Thus in French the nouns referring specifically
to females are always feminine, even though feminine nouns
may refer to males, and in English ONE of the functions of
tense is to refer to time. Indeed it is only because there is some
correlation that the labels 'gender', 'tense', etc., have any use-
fulness at all; the danger is that we should think that such
labels are semantic definitions.

It is, however, as so often in semantics, a mistake to draw
a very clear distinguishing line. As we go into more detailed
investigation of grammar, we find the correlation between
grammar and semantics becomes closer and closer, until we
reach a stage where it is difficult, if not impossible, to declare
whether the categories are formal or semantic. For consider
*John slept coming every day. There are verbs such as *keep*
that are followed by the *-ing* form, e.g. *John kept coming every
day*; others such as *hope* are not, **John hoped coming every
day*. With *hope* the mistake is a grammatical one – we can
correct to *John hoped to come every day*. We might, similarly,
see a grammatical error in *John slept coming every day* in
that *sleep* equally does not occur with an *-ing* form, but it might,
on the other hand, be argued that the anomaly results from
the fact that *sleep* cannot indicate the state of 'coming' as contrasted with *keep* or *begins* which indicate continuity and
initiation, and that the sentence is impossible for semantic
reasons, in that it simply does not 'make sense'. But if we accept

this argument what are we to say of *John ran coming every day*? Does this make sense? If it does not, the restriction is semantic, if it does the restriction is grammatical. But we shall find it very difficult, if not impossible, to decide whether or not it does 'make sense'.

Another example of a borderline case is *John is seeming happy*. We could say this is ungrammatical on the grounds that the verb *seem* does not occur in the progressive (continuous) form *is seeming*. But is this in fact a grammatical rule or is it the case that for semantic reasons John cannot be in a continuous state of seeming? There is no clear answer – the line between grammar and semantics is not a clear one.

The problem we have been discussing is clearly related to the problem of grammar and lexicon that we discussed in the last section. For lexical restrictions are very largely (but see 5.2) determined by semantics. The impossibility, therefore, of drawing a clear line between grammar and lexicon is a corollary of the impossibility of drawing such a line between grammar and semantics.

We find, then, that there are two rather puzzling aspects of the relation between grammar and meaning. First, although we can, and must, set up formal categories, they will be found to have some correlation, but not one-to-one, with semantics. Secondly, we find that there is a difficult borderline area. There is a third point – that some of the major categories seem to be found in all languages. As far as we know, there is no language that does not distinguish in some way between nouns and verbs, even though some may not have different word-classes (parts of speech). All three points can be explained, I believe, by two aspects of language. First, it has a job to do – it has to relate to the world of experience and it would be strange, therefore, if it did not, even in its grammatical system, to some extent reflect the observable features of, e.g., sex, quantity, time, and most importantly, the difference between events and objects. Secondly, however, it is learnt by succeeding generations and is thus to some degree a matter of convention. This accounts for the 'oddity' of *oats* and *wheat* and of the 'female' neuter nouns in German. But it is a characteristic of language at all levels that there are irregularities and exceptions. We find in phonology, for instance, that the sound systems exhibit odd irregularities; e.g. in the 'received pronunciation' of English, [u] (the vowel of *put*) never occurs before [ŋ] (usually spelt *ng*), and the spelling *u* before *ng* always represents [ʌ], the vowel of *cut*. Such irregularities are merely the relics of historical development and accident.

7.3 *Gender and number*

Let us now look briefly at two familiar grammatical categories, gender and number.

We shall not expect to find an exact correlation between gender and sex. Indeed sometimes we have a surprising contrast as in the French of 'the male mouse' which is *la souris mâle* ('the (feminine) male mouse'), for *souris* is a feminine noun. Similarly we noted *Mädchen* and *Fräulein* and *la sentinelle* in the previous section. Yet although in some cases the gender is wholly idiosyncratic, we can at other times see some regularity. The German words are neuter because all words with the diminutive ending *-chen* and *-lein* are neuter, while in French occupational names such as *sentinelle* are all feminine. The explanation then lies in historical facts, which have over-ruled the obvious semantic probability that male creatures will be referred to by masculine nouns and female creatures by feminine ones.

There is no real problem in English, for English has, strictly, no grammatical gender at all. It has, of course, the pronouns *he*, *she* and *it*, but these are essentially markers of sex. The first two, *he* and *she*, are used if the sex is specifically indicated or known; otherwise *it* is used. There is, however, one qualification. There is a difference between the use of the pronouns for animals and for humans. *It* may be used for animals, e.g. to refer to a dog, and so may *he* or *she* if the sex is known. However, with humans *it* cannot be used, even if the sex is unknown. For the indefinite unknown human the forms *they*, *them*, *their* are used in colloquial English (even for singular) as in *Has anyone lost their hat? If anyone comes tell them to go away.* This is frowned on by some grammarians, but seems to me to be a useful and wholly acceptable device for avoiding the indication of sex. For reference to a specific human whose sex is unknown, e.g. a baby, *it* is sometimes used, but it is probably wiser to ask the mother first 'Is it a boy or a girl?'

Many languages have noun classes that function grammatically like the gender classes of the Indo-European and Semitic languages. Thus, in Swahili, there are classes of animates, of small things and of big things, each class clearly indicated formally by an appropriate prefix and requiring agreement with adjectives and verbs. These are often referred to as gender classes. If we are thinking primarily of the grammatical function, that they are classes of nouns that require agreement with adjectives and verbs, the term 'gender' is appropriate, since that is essentially the grammatical function of gender in the more familiar languages. But, of course, it may be argued that some other term that does not suggest a relation with sex should be found (though the purist might be reminded that etymologically gender is not related to sex, but merely means 'kind'). Even with noun classes of the type that are not related to sex we find that there is no precise correspondence between formal class and its meaning. Not all the nouns of the 'small things' class in Swahili are small, while Bloomfield relates that in the Algonquian languages of North America there is a grammatical distinction between animate and inanimate nouns, but that both 'kettle' and 'raspberry' belong to the class of animates, though 'strawberry' is inanimate.

We have similarly noted anomalies with number. Semantically, the question of enumeration does not seem to be a very important one. Many languages have grammatical number systems, but others in various parts of the world (e.g., South-East Asia, West Africa) do not. Moreover, it is difficult to see why SEMANTICALLY the essential distinction should be between singular ('one') and plural ('more than one'). Many languages make this distinction in their grammar, but not all.

Some classical languages – Sanskrit, Greek and Arabic – had, in addition, dual – referring to two objects. Other languages, e.g. Fijian and Tigre (Ethiopia), have distinctions of 'little plurals' and 'big plurals' too. If we look at the problem of counting objectively it is not at all obvious that there are any 'natural' numerical classes that might be expected to be shown in the grammar of all or most languages.

More important, perhaps, is the need to distinguish between individual and mass. This is a distinction that English makes quite clearly, though it is often ignored in the grammar books. The category is referred to as COUNTABILITY, with the noun classes of COUNTABLES and UNCOUNTABLES or COUNT and MASS. Examples of count nouns are *cat* and *book*, while *butter* and *petrol* are mass nouns. Formally the two classes are easily distinguished. Count nouns alone may occur in the singular with the indefinite article *a* – *a cat* (but not **a butter*), while only mass nouns may occur with no article or with the indefinite quantifier *some* (not *some* in the sense of 'some or other') – *Butter is . . . , some butter* (but not **Cat is . . . , *some cat*). Some nouns, e.g. *cake*, *fish* belong to both classes.

The semantic difference between these two classes is clear enough. The count nouns 'individuate' – they indicate individual specimens, while the mass nouns refer to a quantity that is not individuated in this way. But the distinction does not correspond closely to any semantic distinction in the world of experience, and this should be no cause for surprise. It is true that liquids are always referred to by mass nouns because they cannot be individuated. There is no obvious object that can be described as **a water*. But there is no explanation in semantic terms why *butter* is a mass noun while *jelly* is count as well as mass; there is no semantic reason why we can refer to a single mass of jelly as *a jelly* but not to a mass of butter as **a butter*. On the other hand, while *cake* is count as well as mass, for the obvious reason that individual cakes can be recognised, *bread* is only mass – we cannot talk of **a bread*, but have to use a different word, *loaf*. A foreigner could not guess, then, whether such words as *soap*, *trifle*, *cheese* would be count nouns in

English. He has, moreover, to learn the 'individuating' nouns *loaf of bread, cake of soap, pat of butter.*

The count/mass distinction is a fairly clear one – it classifies English nouns, though some, e.g. *fish,* belong to both classes. But mass nouns can, nevertheless, function as count nouns. Two obvious functions are, first, the use of such expressions as *a butter, a petrol* to mean 'a kind of butter' or 'a kind of petrol', and secondly *a coffee, a beer* to mean 'a cup of coffee' and 'a glass of beer'. It is best to treat these nouns as 'basically' mass nouns and these functions as types of individuation that can be applied to them for specific purposes – to indicate kinds and, with liquids, familiar quantities. Similarly, count nouns that refer to creatures may function as mass nouns to indicate the meat; we find not merely familiar usages such as *chicken, rabbit, fish* but can also freely form mass nouns *elephant, crocodile* and even *dog* (*The Chinese eat dog*) to refer to the meat. (But we have, of course, the specific words *beef, mutton, pork, venison* for the flesh of cattle, sheep, pigs and deer.)

Semantically, mass nouns are nearer to plurals than to singular forms of count nouns. This accounts for the anomaly of *oats* and *wheat* – there is little difference, unless it is clearly specified, between a large number of grains and a mass of them. In some languages liquids are not mass nouns, but plurals, e.g. in Bilin the word for 'water'.

The term 'count' is relevant to the fact that most count nouns can be counted – *one book, two/three/four books.* But there are two reservations. First, English has the words *scissors, trousers, shears, tongs,* etc., which are formally plural, but cannot be enumerated except by using another noun *a pair of* —; this is formally like the individuators of the mass nouns, *a cake of soap, a pat of butter.* Secondly, although English uses the plural form with numbers above one, not all languages do. In Welsh, for instance, 'four dogs' is *pedwar ci,* though 'dog' is *ci* and 'dogs' *cwn.* In Tigre there are many mass nouns which have a singulative (individuating) form made by a suffix, e.g. *nəhəb* 'bees', but *nəhbät* 'a bee'. But the singulative form is the form used with all numerals – not merely 'one' *ḥätte nəhbät* 'one bee', *sätäs nəhbät* 'three bees', etc. What seems to be important here is not plurality, but individuation.

7.4 *Person and deixis*

The category of person (first person *I*, *we*, second person *you*, third person *he, she, it, they*) is often closely associated with number and with gender in the verbal forms of languages. (In Western Indo-European languages only number and person are marked in the verb, but in Semitic languages and Eastern Indo-European languages gender is also associated with it.) But person always has a very clear semantic function (unlike gender and, to a lesser extent, number); that function, moreover, is different in that it is DEICTIC (see 2.3), not referring to any general semantic features such as quantity or sex, but to an identifiable item in the context. Thus first person relates to the speaker and second person to the hearer. It follows from this that *I* and *you* have constantly changing reference depending on who is present in the conversation, and are not to be interpreted in terms of any generalisable semantic qualities.

The precise function of any set of person markers, usually the pronouns, but also the endings of verbs in some languages, may vary from language to language, but all can basically be interpreted in terms of speaker, hearer, and those who are non-participants in the conversation or written correspondence, and this is the basis of first, second and third person.

There are some complications. First, languages have plural person markers, and it might be assumed that these refer simply to several speakers, several hearers and several non-participants. But this is not always so. It is rare for there to be several speakers, except in chorus as, for instance, a crowd at a football match crying *We want another* or an impatient group singing *Why are we waiting? We* usually refers not to a plurality of speakers ('I and I and . . .') but to speaker and hearer ('I and you'), speaker and non-participant ('I and he/she') or speaker, hearer and non-participant ('I and you and he/she'), plus any further combinations involving more than one speaker, hearer or non-participant. *You* may well refer to several hearers, but it may also be used to refer to hearer (or hearers) plus non-participant (or non-participants) ('you and he/she', etc.). *They* alone will always refer simply to a number of non-participants. There is in fact a simple rule with the plural: the pronoun is determined by the 'highest' ranking person included. If *I* is included, use *we*; if it is not but *you* is, use *you*; otherwise use *they*. But some languages make other distinctions. Not uncommon are distinct forms for inclusive plural 'I and you' and for exclusive plural 'I and he/she'.

Secondly, there are, in some languages, both a more polite and a less polite form of address. If we take the less polite form as basic we can say that, in the more polite form, instead of the second person singular, the second person plural is used, as in French *vous* for *tu* or that the third person is used instead of the second as in Italian *Lei* for *tu*. If we treat these as different styles of the language we have to say, instead, that in the polite style *vous* is singular as well as plural and *Lei* is second as well as third person. In some cases the 'polite' system has become the only system; thus English has only *you* for singular and plural. But, of course, in modern English it is no longer the case that *you* is polite for *thou*; rather English makes no distinction at all between second person singular and second person plural (though in some dialects, mostly in America, *you all* has become, or is becoming, the plural form, and in others, of course, *thou* still survives).

Person is, then, a deictic category, one that refers to identifiable items in the context. There are other grammatical forms with a similar function. Thus the definite article *the* is used to refer to a single identifiable item in the context, where it is apparent to speaker and hearer precisely what that item is. Thus, although *book* may refer to any book, *the book* refers to a particular book that both speaker and hearer can identify, either one that is being talked about or one that is recognisable in the non-linguistic context, e.g. visible on the table before them. Identification of the item is often simply in terms of the most familiar. *The Government* will usually refer to our government, *the moon* to the moon that we see at night.

Similarly *the kitchen* or *the garden* will refer to our own kitchen or garden, or, if we are in someone else's house, to theirs. But this can change – we may be talking about another government, the moon of another planet or the kitchen and garden of another house. What matters is that the item can be identified in the context without misunderstanding.

Because of its function the article does not normally occur with names (proper nouns). A proper noun such as *Fred, Professor Brown*, etc., is used simply to identify a particular person, and the article would thus be redundant (though it is used, redundantly, in some languages, e.g. Italian). However, even proper nouns are sometimes used in a non-unique sense; thus we can talk about *the three Freds* to mean three people with the name Fred. We can even refer to someone in one of their aspects, e.g. *He's not the Fred I knew*. In such cases we identify a particular Fred or kinds of Fred and the article may be used. There are, however, some idiosyncracies about the use of the article. Thus rivers are identified with the article – *the Severn, the Thames*, etc., but cities are not – *London, Bristol*, etc. (except for *The Hague*). This is a purely formal grammatical point and has no semantic significance.

It is of some interest that if an item becomes uniquely identifiable the article is dropped. Thus we now have *Parliament*, not *the Parliament* and, more surprisingly, perhaps, *Bank rate* and not *the Bank rate*. Since there is only one of each, the noun phrase has, in effect, become a name, a proper noun.

Other deictics are the demonstratives *these* and *those*. No less important are the place adverbs *here, there*, etc., and the time adverbs *now, soon*, etc. For these too do not refer to any particular kind of place or time, but usually to a place or time that can be identified with relation to the speaker and hearer and, less commonly, to time and place identified in the discourse.

What is important about deictics is that they are used to refer to items in the 'context', in the two senses of linguistic and non-linguistic context. Thus the third person *he* may be used to refer to someone already spoken of in the linguistic context

or it may be used (a little impolitely) to refer to someone
actually present. I am informed that in some parts of Britain
it is used by women to refer to their husbands – who else?!
Similarly the definite article *the* may refer to something identifiable either from the linguistic context or the non-linguistic
context or even from the world at large, provided its identity
is not in doubt. Even time and place markers are so used. *Now*
and *here* refer more often than not to the 'now' and 'here' of the
time and place of speaking, but they can be established in
terms of times and places referred to in the discourse.

The moral is clear – if we are to look for contexts to
state meaning we have to look at both linguistic and non-
linguistic context.

7.5 *Transitivity and causativity*

In a detailed discussion of English grammar we should have to
deal with four related categories of the verb, tense, aspect,
phase and voice. These may be illustrated by comparing *plays*
with *played*, *is playing*, *has played* and *is played* respectively.
But voice is rather different from the other three. If we consider *John plays the piano* we can alter tense, phase and aspect
to produce *John played the piano*, *John has played the piano*,
John is playing the piano. With voice the situation is different;
if we want to make the sentence passive, we get either the
nonsensical **John is played (by) the piano*, or we change the
order of the words to produce *The piano is played by John*.

This illustrates the grammatical process now called TRANS-
FORMATION, where the grammatical category affects not just
one element (the verb), but the whole sentence. The passive
transformation is, moreover, possible only with verbs that have
objects, since the object of the active verb becomes the subject
of the passive. We must, however, define the terms subject and
object. At a purely formal level, this provides no difficulty. In
an inflected language, such as Latin, they are clearly marked
by the case system, the subject being in the nominative and the
object in the accusative case (subject to certain grammatical
rules). Thus in *Marcus Julium necavit* 'Marcus killed Julius',

Marcus is in the nominative and *Julium* in the accusative. In English and many other languages the subject and object are marked by position, the subject preceding, the object following, the verb.

There are a few complexities that we should first consider. With some verbs there are indirect as well as direct objects as in *John gave Bill a book* where the direct object is *a book* and the indirect object *Bill*. (In Latin the indirect object is in the dative – *Marcus Julio librum dedit* 'Marcus gave Julius a book', where *Julio* is in the dative.) With these the indirect object may be the subject of the passive, as in *Bill was given a book by John*, as may be the direct object, as in *A book was given to Bill by John* (though this might perhaps be seen as the passive of *John gave a book to Bill* not *John gave Bill a book*). Moreover, we find sentences such as *The old man was looked after by his daughter* in which *the old man* is not strictly the object of the sentence in the active, but is preceded by the preposition *after*; the solution here is to see *look after* as a single verb. More idiosyncratic is *The bed's not been slept in* in which *sleep in* again seems to function as a unit (but contrast the unlikely *★The office's not been worked in*). However, we must obviously make special statements for sentences of this kind. In general, the rule about transformations, which involves movement of subject and object, holds good. Verbs that have objects are called TRANSITIVE, though it must be stressed that this is a grammatical use of the term, quite different from the logical sense of 4.6.

Voice, then, is closely related to grammatical transitivity such that if we regard the verb as indicating a 'transitivity' relation between subject and object, that relation is reversed in the passive. Active and passive are then extremely like the relational opposites we discussed in 4.6.

Transitivity relations of a slightly different kind are also involved in the syntax of some verbs without involving the passive. There are many verbs in English that occur both transitively and intransitively, e.g. *ring* in *John rang the bell* and *The bell rang*. Other such verbs are *open, close, start, stop, cook, boil, break, snap,* etc. With these once again the object of one (the transitive form) is identical with the subject of the other (the intransitive). We shall say more about these in 8.1.

There are some languages that have intransitive and transitive verbs as in English, but indicate the identity of the subject of the intransitive and the object of the transitive verb (*the bell* in both our examples) in a formal way, by putting them both in the same case – the nominative. The other noun, which is the subject of the transitive verb only (*John* in the example), is in the ergative case. The best known of these 'ergative' languages is Basque; others are Eskimo and Georgian, and, in part of their verbal pattern, many of the languages of India.

We can treat English in a similar way if we distinguish between (a) the grammatical subject and object which are marked by position and change with voice and with the transitive/intransitive pairs, and (b) subject and object in a 'deeper' sense, such that both the grammatical subject of the active verb and the agent (preceded by *by*) of the passive are defined as the 'deep subject', while both the grammatical object of the active verb and the grammatical subject of the passive verb are defined as the 'deep object'. Thus *John* is the deep subject and *the piano* the deep object of both *John plays the piano* and *The piano is played by John.*

As long as the terms 'deep subject' and 'deep object' are used to deal solely with formal relations of this kind no real problems arise. But we may well be tempted to see the 'deep' subject as the 'doer' and the 'deep' object as the 'sufferer'; some linguists have used the terms ACTOR and GOAL to make this distinction. There are, however, difficulties if we attempt to define them in semantic terms. For it is by no means true that the subject of a transitive verb can always be seen as one who 'does' something. There are many verbs in English that are not verbs of action but verbs of state, e.g. *like* in *I like ice cream* or even *see* in *I saw the boys.* Indeed with some of these verbs we should not usually ask *What did he do?* (though this, contrary to what some linguists have suggested, is not a very clear test, as the reader can judge for himself with *like* and *see*). With some of the verbs of perception, moreover, we have pairs of 'state' and 'action' verbs. Alongside *see* we have *look at* and alongside *hear*, *listen to*. It is only with *look at* and *listen to* that the subject is doing anything. (The other verbs of perception *smell*, *feel* and *taste* have no 'companion' verb, but can all be used in both a 'state' and an 'action' sense.)

Verbs of this kind should deter us from attempting to define *actor* in semantic terms. But even with action verbs, it is not clear that we can clearly establish what is meant by *actor*. For instance, M. A. K. Halliday quotes as an example of an actor *General Leathwell* in the sentence *General Leathwell won the battle*. But in what sense is he the actor? Did he fire any guns, kill any enemy, advance to the enemies' lines, or did he merely sit in his HQ and let the troops get on with the battle? We could surely argue that semantically he was not the actor, but the 'supervisor'!

It is difficult, if not impossible, then to define *actor* and *goal* in purely semantic terms. In fact, the apparently semantic definitions are probably circular – based upon, first, selection of the active of many common verbs (the 'action' verbs) being typical and, secondly, that these verbs can usually be referred to with *do*. Actor and goal are thus no more than the deep subject and object of the most 'typical' verbs of English.

Closely related to transitivity is causativity. Indeed some linguists have been tempted to analyse transitive sentences as essentially causative ones. That is to say *John rang the bell* is to be interpreted as 'John caused the bell to ring'. Using predicate calculus, we may thus interpret the sentence as [Cause] John, ([Ring] bell), rather than as [Ring] John, bell. This will bring out the relations between our transitive and intransitive pairs, by making all verbs intransitive in this more abstract analysis. But there are objections to this. First, we need to make a distinction between transitive and causative verbs. For consider *The sergeant marched the recruits*. Although we also have *The recruits marched* there is a difference between these sentences and the *ring* pair in that the recruits, unlike the bell, are semantically actors or agents, performing the action by their own will and effort. The sergeant is then a 'causer' in a rather different and more obvious sense than *John* in *John rang the bell*. Secondly, there are many verbs that do not lend themselves easily to a translation into causative terms. *Ring* may be seen as 'cause to ring' and *kill* as 'cause to die', but what of *hit*? We may see *John killed Bill* as 'John caused Bill to die' but *John hit Bill* is 'John caused Bill to — (?)'.

This is not to suggest that there is a clear distinction semantically between transitivity and causativity. Evidence for this comes from the variation in different languages. The English intransitive and transitive *cook* are translated in French by *cuire* and *faire cuire* (which is clearly causative), and there are many other such verbs. There are languages in which the distinction is made formally, in that besides active and passive forms they have causative forms of the verb, but the formal distinction does not seem to relate to a semantic one. For instance, in the Ethiopian languages 'to kill' is an active transitive verb, but 'to bounce' is the causative of an intransitive verb 'to bounce' or 'to jump'. But why, then, is 'to kill' not the causative of 'to die'? There is no obvious semantic reason. More surprisingly, perhaps, in Classical Greek 'to die' functions as the passive of 'to kill'. (One can 'die BY someone'.) Formally, at least, Greek treats 'to kill', not 'to die', as the more basic.

It is clear from all the discussion in this section that we can see no clear correspondence between formally established relations of transitivity and semantics. But we shall return to the problem immediately in 8.1.

8

RECENT ISSUES

In this chapter I wish to discuss some topics that have been of particular interest to linguists in recent years. Some of them are related to topics dealt with in previous chapters, but their importance lies in their topicality rather than in the position they hold in semantics. In the brief space of a single chapter, it is naturally impossible to deal with the issues fully. I can do no more than present brief outlines and point out some of the difficulties.

8.1 *Case relations*

We discussed the problem of subject and object in 7.5. One attempt to deal with the semantics of such categories is to be found in 'case theory' associated with C. J. Fillmore.

We begin by considering a trio of sentences such as *John opened the door with a key, The key opened the door* and *The door opened*. There is the same verb, *open*, in all three, and in all three it is active. Yet the grammatical subjects are *John, the key* and *the door* respectively. Fillmore suggests that these facts can be accounted for if we handle *John, the key* and *the door* in terms of 'case relations' that are not directly related to grammatical subject and object, the case of each noun being the same in all three sentences. Thus *John* is AGENTIVE (='actor') throughout, *the key* is INSTRUMENTAL and *the door* is OBJEC-TIVE. We can now state that nouns in any of these three cases, agentive, instrumental or objective may be the grammatical subject. With an active verb, however, which of them is to function as subject is determined by a simple rule of precedence that sets the cases in the order agentive, instrumental, objective. That is to say, if the agentive is present (*John*) it will always be the subject – *John opened the door with a key*, but not **The key opened the door by John* or **The door opened with a key by John*. Similarly if there is an instrumental but no agentive, the instrumental will be the subject – *The key opened the door*, but not **The door opened with a key*. Only if the objective is alone can it be the subject – *The door opened*.

As a means of relating sentences such as these case grammar works well. We could easily produce a comparable set with *ring* – *John rang the bell with a hammer*, *The hammer rang the bell*, *The bell rang*. In identifying agentive, instrumental and objective we should be merely developing the notions of 'actor' and 'goal' (or 'deep' subject and object) that were suggested in 7.5. What is new is that we are not concerned solely with active and passive sentences, but in addition with trios such as those we have illustrated, and that we need a further category, instrumental (for agentive and objective can be identified with actor and goal). But the categories would still be formal – based only on relations of a transformational kind between sentences.

Fillmore's proposals go far beyond this. He suggests rather that his case notions are 'a set of universal, presumably innate, concepts' and proceeds to define them in semantic terms. To begin with he suggests six cases, Agentive ('typically animate perceived instigator'), Instrumental ('inanimate force or object causally involved'), Dative ('animate being affected'), Factitive ('object or being resulting from the action or state'), Locative ('location or spatial orientation'), Objective ('the semantically most neutral case').

On the basis of such definitions (I have quoted only the most relevant parts), Fillmore proceeds to suggest what cases are required for other verbs. Thus *kill* must have a dative and either an agent or an instrumental or both. (The person killed is indicated by the dative, since he is the animate affected, and the killing is obviously done by an animate (Agentive) or inanimate (Instrumental) or both – *The man killed him*, *The rock killed him*, *The man killed him with a rock*.) *Die* involves only a dative. Similarly *show* needs agentive, dative and objective (one shows something to somebody), while *see* requires dative and objective. There is a contrast between *see* and *look* (*at*), in that the latter requires agentive and objective (with *look* the person takes an active part, with *see* he is merely affected).

Although case theory has some initial plausibility, there are grave difficulties with it. To begin with, if the cases are defined semantically, we shall have all the usual problems of the vagueness of semantic definition. Let us consider first the distinction between agentive and instrumental. Fillmore suggests that the agentive is 'typically animate', but we can always invent examples where there are two inanimate objects involved, e.g. *The storm broke the glass with the hailstones.* We must assume, therefore, that although agents are usually animate, animateness is not an essential part of the definition. But if so, we soon find borderline cases. For, if *John* may be agentive in *John broke the window* and *the rock* instrumental in *The rock broke the window*, it is not easy to see why *the wind* should be instrumental rather than agentive in *The wind broke the window, The wind rustled the leaves* or why *John* should be agentive if he broke the window accidentally or as a result of someone pushing him. Similarly, there are problems with other cases. Part of Fillmore's argument, it will be recalled, was that the choice of subject of a sentence was determined by certain 'formal' grammatical rules rather than the more 'notional' case. He argues that the same is true of the direct objects and illustrates this with comparison of *present something to someone* and *present someone with something.* Presumably he wishes to say that, although the direct object is *something* in the first sentence and *someone* in the second, this is unrelated to case for *something* is objective and *someone* is dative in both examples. Thus this analysis probably results from taking the first example as basic – where objective and dative are identical with object and indirect object, and then proceeding to the argument that the same cases hold for the second example because of its similar meaning and in spite of the difference in its form. But why should we not, instead, argue that the second example is to be treated in terms of objective (*someone*) and instrumental (*something*) as the surface form suggests? (Or, perhaps, dative and instrumental, since someone is animate?) For if we want to establish the semantics we might ask whether *present someone with something* is like *reward someone with something* or *punish someone with something*. And are these not close to *beat someone with something*? We are faced once again with a problem that is typical of semantics – where to draw a line between what at first seemed to be quite distinct categories.

There are also many distinctions that case grammar cannot handle. Again we may take Fillmore's own examples: *John smeared paint on the wall/John smeared the wall with paint. Bees are swarming in the garden/The garden is swarming with bees.* In each pair the cases would have to be the same for *John, paint, wall, bees,* and *garden,* but the meanings of the sentences are not the same. Similarly, the verbs *buy* and *sell* seem to involve the same cases – and indeed part of the attraction of case grammar is that they do – yet *John bought a book from Mary* is not the same as *Mary sold John a book.* These examples suggest quite strongly that there is some function of the grammatical subject that makes these paired sentences different. Fillmore admits this, but argues that we can only investigate the function of the subject, if we are clear about the case-functions. But this is an odd conclusion. Was not the argument in favour of case the fact that grammatical subject has no consistent function?

8.2 *Performatives and speech acts*

In a famous little book (edited and published after his death) *How to do things with words* the Oxford philosopher, J. L. Austin, pointed out that there are a number of utterances that do not report or 'constate' anything and are not therefore 'true or false', but rather that the uttering of the sentence is, or is part of, an action. Examples are *I name this ship Queen Elizabeth, I bet you sixpence it will rain tomorrow.* By uttering such sentences the speaker actually names the ship or makes the bet, but he is not making any kind of statement that can be regarded as true or false. The sentences that he is concerned with here are all grammatically statements but they are not CONSTATIVE, they are PERFORMATIVE. Austin includes along with the performative sentences (or simply performatives) *I promise . . .* and suggests that one can find a list of performative verbs incuding *apologise, thank, censure, approve, congratulate.* With all of these a sentence with *I* and a present tense verb will be an example of a performative.

He proceeds, however, to distinguish these performatives as EXPLICIT performatives in contrast with the IMPLICIT performatives which do not contain an expression naming the act. We can achieve the same end with *Go* as with *I order you to go* and similarly *There is a bull in the field* may (or may not) be a warning, while *I shall be there* may (or may not) be a promise. This leads to the distinction between a LOCUTIONARY ACT and an ILLOCUTIONARY ACT. In the locutionary act we are 'saying something' but we may also use the locution for particular purposes – to answer a question, to announce a verdict, to give a warning, etc. In this sense we are performing an illocutionary act. This led Austin and others who followed to talk of SPEECH ACTS, the classification of utterances in terms of promises, warnings, etc., and even, finally, to the recognition that making statements (constatives) are but one kind of speech act.

There is something in common here with Malinowski's view of language as a 'mode of action' (3.2) and it is a welcome reminder that meaning is not to be identified with cognitive meaning. But there are some clear differences and difficulties. Within the discussion of speech acts there is always the assumption that the sentence has a propositional meaning (is a locutionary act) as well as being an illocutionary act in the act of stating, warning, ordering, apologising, etc.; Malinowski, of course, argued that language was 'a mode of action *not a countersign of thought*'. Moreover, there is a world of difference between a performative such as *I name this ship Queen Elizabeth* and the speech act of warning involved in *There is a bull in the field*. The former is controlled firmly by convention and ritual – the act of naming is not achieved without it. The latter is not part of any conventional behaviour and it is not at all clear under what circumstances it is a warning. For example, is it a warning if I intend it to be, but it is not so understood? With the true performative the act IS achieved by the words alone, but with a 'speech act' such as a warning this is not necessarily so.

We can, in fact, distinguish a number of different kinds of linguistic phenomena which are related but are not quite the same. How far the term performative is applicable to them all is debatable.

First, we have some of the examples with which Austin began. *I name this ship Queen Elizabeth* has two clear characteristics. To begin with, it is part of an action, that of christening a ship; further, it begins with *I* plus a present tense verb, which names the action while performing it. A similar example (in writing, not speech) is *I give and bequeath my watch to my brother*.

Secondly, there are many utterances that do not contain *I* plus a present tense verb that are, nevertheless, 'performatives' in the sense that they are essentially part of an action. Examples are the calls in bridge *Three clubs*, *No bid*, etc., or the call in cricket *No ball*. For uttering the bridge call binds the speaker to that contract, while in cricket the umpire's *No ball* makes the delivery a 'no ball' in the sense that the batsman cannot now be out by being bowled, stumped, caught or l.b.w.

Thirdly, there are the utterances that begin *I promise . . .* , *I warn . . .* , *I promise to come tomorrow*, *I warn you that there is a bull in the field*. These are performatives in that they are to be seen as the action of promising, warning, etc., and that the action is named by the verb (and with both *I* and a present tense verb again). But they differ from the first type of performative in that (a) they are not part of any conventional or ritual behaviour, and (b) the performative verb may be omitted without the loss of the illocutionary force; the naming of the action does not seem to be an absolute requirement (but see on the fifth type, below). We can promise without using the verb *promise*, but we cannot christen a ship without using the verb *name*. Similarly, we may compare *warn* with *bet* as in *I bet you sixpence it will rain tomorrow*. The bet is not 'on' unless the words *I bet . . .* are used. *I bet . . .* then is a performative in the earlier stricter sense, in that the performative verb is an essential element and cannot be omitted.

Fourthly, the modal verbs *shall* and *may/can* are used to make promises and give permission (and *must* to lay obligation). Austin mentions *I shall come tomorrow* as an example of an implicit performative, but we can argue that there is nothing implicit about *You shall have it tomorrow, You can go now*. These are clearly and unambiguously a promise and a granting of permission. The meaning is explicitly stated by the modal verb, though it is not a performative verb in the strict sense.

Fifthly, we have the fact that *There is a bull in the field* may be a warning or a boast or simply the giving of a piece of information. It is this last type of utterance that has largely interested philosophers. But this fifth type is different from all the others and raises problems that they do not. To begin with there is no overt indication of the kind of speech act involved. This means that it is very difficult in practice to determine whether a particular utterance is to be characterised as a particular kind of speech act. Even the speaker may not have a clear idea of his own intentions. He may say *There is a bull in the field* because he is a little afraid for his companions, but is that enough to constitute a warning? People's intentions and purposes are often far from clear even to themselves – yet the notion of speech act seems at least to require that we know the use to which the utterance is being put. Then, we must decide how many kinds of speech acts we can establish. It seems reasonable to recognise a type of the speech act if there is an actual performative verb in the language, and this has been the assumption in most discussions. Thus we recognise warnings and promises as speech acts because we have the verbs *warn* and *promise,* and Austin suggested that the number of performative verbs was in the order of four figures (the 'third power of ten' he said). But we must surely doubt whether the existence of a list of verbs in a dictionary can provide the list of possible types of speech acts. The layman admittedly can only report as speech acts those for which he has an appropriate verb, but it does not seem to follow that the linguist or philosopher should recognise as speech acts only those that the language allows the layman to report. Moreover, it would follow that if French has a different set of such verbs (not corresponding to those of English), we shall have to recognise a different set of speech acts.

It should be noticed, too, that a speech act may not coincide with an actual performative function. Thus, if I say *Double* in bridge, I have performatively committed myself to a particular contract, but I may well do so simply in order to warn my partner or invite him to proceed further. I may even use a performative verb as in *I promise to do it*, yet be performing the speech act of a warning or a threat. Yet curiously the notion of speech act has been derived from the notion of performative. We are, indeed, on uncertain ground here.

Some linguists have made a different and much more limited use of Austin's notion of performative, but not, I believe, with any great success. It is usual in grammar to see three kinds of sentence, statements, questions and commands, or, in more technical terms, declarative, interrogative and imperative sentences. There are clear formal marks of these types, the interrogative being marked by inversion of the subject and verb and the imperative by omission of the subject (as well as by having no tense). Thus we can have no doubts about the status of:

> *John shut the door.*
> *Did John shut the door?*
> *Shut the door.*

We have already noted that the interrogative and, more especially, the imperative raise problems for interpretation in terms of cognitive meaning. Some linguists have avoided (or ignored) this problem by treating all these three types of sentence as essentially the same, except for an element that indicates their interrogative or imperative status. Thus in one form of grammar the markers Q (=question) and Imp (=imperative) are inserted and the problem is solved! A more extreme view sees the difference in terms of abstract ('underlying') performative verbs such that *Did John shut the door?* is interpreted in terms of *I ask you whether John shut the door* and *Shut the door* in terms of *I order you to shut the door* (to be fair, these are merely paraphrases, to indicate what the underlying abstract structures are intended to indicate). It is but a small step to see that *John shut the door* can be seen as *I state that John shut the door*, so that ALL sentences have an underlying performative verb.

I shall not discuss this in detail. It adds nothing to our knowledge of syntax or semantics and is open to fairly obvious objections. First, it puts the cart before the horse. Sentences beginning *I state . . . , I ask . . . , I order . . .* are reports of statements, questions and commands and are rightly seen in the traditional grammar books as indirect statements, questions and commands; they are derived from the direct ones and not vice versa. Secondly, it is abundantly clear that the meaning is not the same. To give an order is not the same as to specify that one is giving an order. Thirdly, this is, in effect, to reduce all sentences to a single type – that of the statement, but there is no advantage in so doing. Language consists of orders, questions, etc., as well as statements as both Austin and his successors so clearly pointed out. Nothing is gained by attempting to disguise the quite different types by reducing them all to one.

There is, moreover, a problem of delimiting the number of sentence types required. For it might seem reasonable to treat *John's coming?* with a rising intonation as an interrogative (notice that the punctuation suggests that it is). But once we introduce intonation as evidence of sentence type, we have no stopping point. For we CAN ask questions with different intonations and we can, of course, suggest, make implications, suggestions, etc., with the appropriate intonation tune. There may seem to be a good case for saying that we should classify sentence types in terms of intonation, since this would be to approach the problem of speech acts from the formal side, for intonation is part of the form of the language. But, if we do, we shall have a multitude of types, since intonation is so varied. If we do not, we are limited to the narrow bounds of the three traditional types, declarative, interrogative and imperative, marked purely by formal (but not including intonational) features.

8.3 *Topic and comment*

Czech linguists (notably J. Firbas) have for a number of years been interested in Functional Sentence Perspective or FSP, for short. In particular, they have distinguished in the sentence between THEME and RHEME, or what has in most other schools of linguistics been called TOPIC and COMMENT. This stems from the idea that we can distinguish between what we are talking about (the topic) and what we are saying about it (the comment). In some languages, there are formal ways of distinguishing topic and comment – and the category is thus a formal one. One way in which the distinction may be made is by the order of the words, and this is the situation in Czech where the theme, what is being talked about, is placed in initial position in the sentence.

If a language has clear markers of topic and comment, the linguistic description raises few problems, for the categories are formally marked and it is always relatively easy to give semantic descriptions to formal categories. But English and many other languages have no simple formal category and it is then not clear what might be meant by *topic* and *comment*. Indeed in English there seem to be at least four features that can be related to the notion.

First, it is possible in English to place a word at the beginning of a sentence when this is not its normal syntactic position as in *The man over there I do not like very much*. This is a device for indicating first what we are going to talk about, and is thus reasonably treated as an example of topicalisation. But it is a fairly rare phenomenon in English. We do not usually place words or phrases initially for this purpose. Moreover, if this is topic, it is marked only if the words or phrases are NOT in their normal positions.

Secondly, we can often choose alternative syntactic constructions whose chief difference lies in what is the subject. An obvious example is active and passive, *John hit Bill* and *Bill was hit by John*. More complex are *This violin is easy to play sonatas on, Sonatas are easy to play on this violin*. It is argued that the choice is determined by topicalisation, the construction chosen being the one which brings the topic into subject position. But it is by no means clear that *John* and *Bill, the violin* and *sonatas* are in any independent semantic sense the topic, what is being talked about. We are simply defining topic in terms of being the subject, in which case the semantics of topicalisation are simply the semantics of being the subject. But can we even find some clear motivation for the choice of one construction rather than another with particular reference to the choice of the subject? There are, perhaps, two reasons for choosing the passive. First, it is often a matter of the 'cohesion' of the discourse to retain the same subject – *The child ran into the road and was hit by a car* shows a little more 'cohesion' than *The child ran into the road and a car hit him*. Secondly, the passive is used where the 'doer' is unknown as in *The child was knocked down,* or where it is deliberately left unstated. This is characteristic of scientific reports where the reporter uses the passive to avoid reference to himself, e.g. *The water was heated to 80°C*. But the first of these is little more than a stylistic device, and the second is a direct result of the grammar of English which always requires a sentence to have a subject. Only in a very vague sense, then, is choice of construction involving the subject a matter of topicalisation.

Thirdly, English has clear devices for dealing with the 'given' and the 'new', the information that is already known in the discourse and the information that is being freshly stated. English has several ways of making the distinction. We can avoid restating in detail what is given by using pronouns – the third person pronouns *he/she/it/they* instead of the already mentioned *the little boy, the man on the corner,* etc. Not only are there pronouns, there are also pro-verbs, e.g. *do* as in *John came early and so did Fred,* and there are, similarly, 'pro-form' adjectives, adverbs and conjunctions – *such, so, therefore,* etc. All of these refer back to something already stated, which is not, therefore, to be stated in full again. We also use sentence stress or accent for a similar purpose, the general rule being that the accent, the point at which there is a fall or a rise, will be on the last item that is new; whatever follows is given and is by this means not highlighted. Thus in *John hit Bill and then Fréd hit him* the accent falls on *Fred* since that alone is new, *hit* and *him* being part of what is given. In contrast in *John saw Bill and then Fred hit him* the accent will fall on *hit,* for *hit* is now new. Even more strikingly, we can place the accent on *him* in *John hit Bill and then Fred hit hím* to mean that Fred hit John not Bill. The explanation is that, though *John* is not strictly new, it is new as the goal rather than the actor. The given, incidentally, may be given from the general, non-linguistic context, not the linguistic discourse. Thus in *The kettle's boiling* the accent usually falls on *kettle* simply because *boiling* is uninformative. There is nothing new, for what else could the kettle be doing?

Fourthly, we often use accent for contrast. In *John hit Bill* any one of the three words may be accented. But this is not merely to topicalise, but to contrast. We are not merely talking about John, hitting or Bill, but we are saying that it was John and not someone else, hitting and not something else, Bill and not someone else. There is a similar, though more striking use, with *not,* where the accent 'picks' out what or who 'is not'; in contrast with what or who 'is'. Thus we can accent various words in *The professors didn't sign the petition* to suggest that others did, that they did something other than sign, or that they signed something else. The same semantic effect can often be achieved by using the paraphrase *It was . . .,* *It was John who hit Bill, It wasn't the professors who signed the petition* (for the verb we have to say *What John did was to hit*

Bill). But such paraphrases are not always possible, e.g. with
a contrasted adjective or adverb – *He's not a cruél man, He
didn't run fást,* for we cannot say **It isn't cruel that he's a man,
It isn't fast that he ran. Moreover, we can accent parts of
words – *They didn't dénationalise (They renationalised), This
isn't a Sémitic language (It's Hamitic).* No paraphrase at all
is possible here. Some scholars have attempted to analyse the
accentual features in terms of the paraphrase. Clearly this is
misguided.

   We have, then, at least four different phenomena that may be
handled under topic and comment. All are in their own way
part of the semantics of the language.

8.4 *Presupposition*

Philosophers have for a long time been concerned with the
semantic status of an expression such as *The King of France,*
if there is no King of France, if, that is to say, there is nothing
to which it refers in the strict sense of reference. In particular
they have asked whether it is correct to say that *The King of
France is bald* is a false statement.

   One solution to the problem, discussed by Strawson, is to
say that in using such expressions, 'referring expressions',
which are grammatically definite noun phrases, the speaker
assumes that the hearer can identify the person or thing referred to. He does not thereby ASSERT that the item exists but
merely presumes that the hearer knows what it is. It is thus
no part of the assertion, but of the PRESUPPOSITION.

   Linguists have recently become interested in presupposition.
Unfortunately some have confused the issue by speaking of
presupposition in terms of 'the speaker's and hearer's beliefs'
as opposed to what is true or false. This is misleading for two
reasons. First, we must always assume, that, unless he is
deliberately misleading, the speaker believes what he asserts
as much as what he presupposes. Secondly, we are never interested in the linguistic behaviour of individual speakers. It
would be of no relevance that someone believed that *sheep*

refers to cows. The status, then, of presuppositions must be no different from that of any other kind of meaning; it is no more concerned with the beliefs of individual speakers and hearers.

We must look rather for clear objectively identifiable distinctions in the language. One such set is to be found in what have been called the 'factive predicates'. We may contrast *It is significant that John came early*, with *It is likely that John came early*, and similarly *I regret that she said it* with *I suppose that she said it*. In the first of each pair the statement in the subordinate ('that') sentence is presupposed – *John came early, She said it*; in the second it is not.

It has been claimed, moreover (by e.g. E. Keenan), that what is presupposed can be identified by the fact that presuppositions are 'preserved under negation', that is to say that they are logically implied by both a positive sentence and its negative counterpart. Thus *It isn't significant that John came early* still implies that *John came early* and *I don't regret that she said it* still implies *She said it*. What then is implied by both the positive and the negative sentence is established as the presupposition.

Presupposition holds, it is argued, for a variety of types. It is clear with all kinds of noun phrase. *John married (didn't marry) Fred's sister* implies Fred had a sister; *John was (wasn't) worried by his wife's infidelity* implies his wife was unfaithful. There are other kinds too. *The lecturer continued (didn't continue) speaking* implies that the lecturer was speaking and *He drank (didn't drink) another glass of beer* implies that he drank at least one glass. It is even claimed that *She cleaned (didn't clean) the room* implies the room was dirty.

Unfortunately the negation test does not work. In *John was/ wasn't worried about his wife's infidelity* it is suggested that what is presupposed is that his wife was unfaithful. But this is not necessarily true of the negative *John was not worried about his wife's infidelity*, since this could be taken to mean either that she was unfaithful but that he was not worried, or that he was not worried BECAUSE she was not unfaithful. In other words the negative can negate what is allegedly the pre-supposition as well as the assertion, and the negative test fails.

The fact that there is no simple negative test is clear enough from a reading of the discussion by philosophers about presupposition. Let us return to *The King of France*. It was suggested, on the one hand, that when there is 'reference failure' (there is no King of France) it might be appropriate to say that *The King of France is bald* is not false, but is neither true nor false and simply has a 'truth value gap'. Yet, on the other hand, *This exhibition was visited by the King of France* is more reasonably regarded as false, not as lacking truth value. For we can say *The exhibition wasn't visited by the King of France because there is no King of France*. Yet it can easily be seen that the two sentences are not really different. For we can equally say *The King of France isn't bald, because there is no King of France*. In other words, if use of the term *The King of France is bald* presupposes that there is a King of France, the negative *The King of France isn't bald* does not necessarily 'preserve' the presupposition, but may actually deny it. In every case, in fact, it is possible to negate the sentences by denying the presupposition. Thus there is nothing odd about *He didn't continue speaking, because he didn't speak at all* or *He didn't drink another glass of beer, because he didn't drink any at all*. Indeed we may recall the Mad Hatters' invitation to Alice to take some more tea. Her reply was to deny the presupposition that she had had some, 'I've had nothing yet, so I can't take more'. Lewis Carroll certainly knew that presuppositions do not hold under negation!

This shows that there is no way of distinguishing, in precise logical terms, between what is asserted and what is presupposed. It does not, however, invalidate the distinction entirely. It is normally very clear indeed what is asserted and what is presupposed. In particular the 'existence' of everything referred to by a noun phrase is usually presupposed – not only 'referring expressions' such as *The King of France*, but also nominal clauses (which have the grammatical status of noun phrases) such as *that John came early* (except where the verb, e.g. *believe*, specifically indicates that there is a question about its 'existence', i.e. whether it is or is not true). Some scholars (apparently wishing to avoid the logical connotations of 'presupposition') have preferred to talk not about 'presupposition' here but 'implicatives', but if there are no logically definable presuppositions, there is no need for another name.

8.5 *Generative semantics*

The controversy about formal and semantic grammar that was discussed in 7.2 has been revived in a new form in recent years in terms of 'interpretive' and 'generative' semantics. It is impossible to do justice to the discussion of this in this book since it is to a large extent a technical one within the theory of transformational-generative grammar. But since it is of topical interest, something must be said, though it will inevitably be rather superficial.

It will be recalled (7.5) that in the discussion of active and passive sentences it was necessary to talk about 'deep' subjects and objects which remain the same even though the order of words is changed when a sentence is 'passivised'. Chomsky argued, in fact, that there is a syntactic DEEP STRUCTURE and that it is at this level that we can relate active and passive sentences, and, indeed, that the only difference between an active and its related passive sentence would be the absence or presence of an element *passive*. Thus *John played the piano* is to be analysed in terms of *John, play, past tense, the piano* while *The piano was played by John* is to be analysed in terms of *John, play, past tense, the piano* and *passive*. (This is a grossly over-simplified account, but illustrates the points that are relevant here.) Similarly, we can relate the statement *John is coming* and the question *Is John coming?* in terms of the presence or absence of Q (Question). The difference in the order of the words (as well as other differences) in the paired sentences is a matter of their SURFACE STRUCTURE.

In the examples we have considered so far the surface structures are very different, but the deep structures are similar and differ only in the presence or absence of a single element. There are other pairs of sentences with similar surface structures but quite different deep structures. One well-known pair is *John is eager to please* and *John is easy to please*. The deep structures will have to indicate that *John* is the deep subject of *please* in the first and the object of *please* in the second, and also that while *John* is the subject of *is* in the first, the subject of *is* is '— please John' in the second. Very roughly, we need deep structures to suggest *John is eager* (*John please* —) and (— *please John*) *is easy* (the blanks indicating unstated subjects and objects).

Part of the syntax is concerned with rules that convert deep structures into surface structures. It is essential, of course, that given the deep structure these rules will AUTOMATICALLY generate the correct surface structure. The deep structure rules are themselves generated by the BASE which consists of two components – the CATEGORIAL COMPONENT and the LEXICON. The former contains the whole of the grammatical apparatus and the latter the inventory of all the lexical items. Thus the deep structures will contain all the necessary grammatical and all the necessary lexical information. Thus to return to our first pair of examples, we need to know not only that we have the lexical items *John, play, piano,* but also the grammatical status of *John* and *the piano* as noun phrases and play as a verb (for without this we might generate such non-sentences as *The piano is Johnned by play*). The first set of information is provided by the lexicon, the second by the categorial component of the base.

A further claim is made for deep structure – that it provides the source of the semantic interpretation. Given, that is to say, the grammatical and lexical information that the deep structure of a sentence provides, we can in theory say what that sentence means.

This is a very neat model of syntax. We have a level in the syntax at which the relevant information will lead both to the meaning and the surface structure of a sentence (Chomsky goes on, incidentally, to improve the symmetry of the model by arguing that the surface structure will provide the phonetic interpretation).

Other scholars, however, have argued that we cannot establish such a level – that there is, therefore, no deep structure, or that, if there is a deep structure, it is not syntactic but semantic – that the only deep structure is the semantics. The arguments are many and rather complex. I will consider a few of them.

The first is in Fillmore's case. The arguments relating *The door opened*, *The key opened the door* and *John opened the door* are very similar to those that relate active and passive sentences, and it would seem to follow, therefore, that if active and passive can be used to establish deep structure, these sentences can be used in the same way and that, therefore, deep structure should be in terms of case relations. But, as we saw, case relations are more semantic than syntactic, and deep structure must, therefore, not be merely 'deeper' than Chomsky had supposed, but also semantic rather than syntactic.

The second argument (by J. McCawley) is a little more technical but fairly simple. It has always been assumed in transformational-generative grammar that sentences such as *John and Bill like ice-cream* are derived by CONJOINING, relating to the sentences *John likes ice-cream* and *Bill likes ice-cream*. A single sentence in surface structure must then be derived from two sentence structures in deep structure. (This is again an over-simplification of what Chomsky said.) The sentence *John and Bill love their respective wives* must similarly be analysed in terms of *John loves his wife* and *Bill loves his wife*. But we can also say *Those men love their respective wives*. This cannot, however, be generated in the same way because it would involve a completely unspecified number of deep structure sentences *That man loves his wife* and *That man loves his wife* and . . . . The number of deep structure sentences might even be infinite as with *All whole numbers are smaller than their respective squares*. To account for sentences of this kind, it is argued that we need a deep structure that is nearer a logical structure – one that says, e.g. 'for each *y* such that *y* is the wife of *x*, *x* loves *y*'. But in that case we shall have handled the phenomena associated with *respective* in two places in the grammar and the postulation of deep structure, it is argued, will 'split' the relevant generalisation. (If the reader finds the sentences unnatural because of *respective*, this word can be omitted, but the argument still holds provided that the meaning is unchanged, i.e. that it is still understood that each man loves his own wife.)

Thirdly, the deep structure analysis of the active/passive relationship seems to break down with *Many men read few books* and *Few books are read by many men*. For these are clearly different in meaning. The first says that lots of men read very little, but the second that there are few books (e.g. the Bible, Shakespeare) that are read by a lot of people. There is a similar difference between *Many arrows didn't hit the target* and *The target wasn't hit by many arrows*. To analyse such pairs of sentences as having the same deep structure, except for the presence of the passive marker, is clearly most unsatisfactory. The deep structures, it is argued (G. Lakoff), must be the semantic structures, which, in effect, say, 'The men who read few books are many' and 'The books that many men read are few'.

There are three ways in which these arguments can be countered. First, it can be pointed out that merely to show that there are semantic structures is not to prove that there are no syntactic deep structures. On the contrary, these semantic structures merely provide the semantic interpretation for the deep structures. This is the line that Chomsky takes with Fillmore's case. In so far as Fillmore's cases are defined semantically, it is a fair reply – the 'case' interpretation of *kill* can be seen simply as the semantics of that word. The reply is less valid with the case relations established on more formal grounds for *open*, and it might be reasonable to accept case here as a 'deeper' deep structure – yet that deep structure would still be syntactic for these case relations rest on formal syntactic, not semantic, criteria.

Secondly, however, some deep structure solutions may have

to be abandoned. Conjoining does not seem to be a satisfactory solution for the sentences involving *respective*. But this merely reduces the scope of deep structure, it does not deny its existence.

Thirdly, Chomsky has been forced to change his model in one respect – that he now allows surface structure to provide part of the semantic interpretation. This is a result of consideration of sentences such as *Few books are read by many men*. For while deep structure can deal with *books*, *read* and *men* (in terms of *men read books* and *passive*), it cannot handle *few* and *many* at the same level for this would suggest that this sentence is identical in meaning with *Many men read few books*. Chomsky, therefore, suggests that for 'quantifiers' such as *many* and *few* the surface structure order is important and that the semantic interpretation of this can only be obtained from the surface structure. Unfortunately, this solution seems to be an effort to 'patch up' the model, for the original arguments in favour of deep structure would demand that the two sentences differ in deep structure.

There is one further issue that is part of the generative/interpretive controversy, but is concerned more with the status of the lexical aspect of deep structure. It will be recalled that the base consists of a categorial component and a lexical component, that these generate the deep structures, and that only after this are the deep structures converted to surface structures by transformational rules. But others have argued that the lexical items themselves are to be derived by transformational rules and not directly supplied in the base by the lexical component. If this is so, there can be no single independent level of deep structure, for it is essential, on the theory, that transformations follow and never precede deep structures. One such argument is based upon the verb *kill* which, it is suggested, has to be analysed as 'cause . . . to become not alive'. This is supported by the triple ambiguity of *I almost killed him*, where, it is argued, *almost* may qualify *cause*, *become* or *not alive*. The first sense applies if I shot at him, but missed (I almost caused the subsequent events, but did not). The second applies if I hit him and he recovered after narrowly avoiding death (he almost became dead). The third applies if I shot him and he was in a state of near death (he became almost dead). On the basis of this it is argued that *kill* must be interpreted in terms of three sentences in deep structure (and these would correspond to the three propositions of predicate calculus, see 6.3).

But once again there is the reply that to prove that there are semantic complexities of this kind associated with lexical items does not prove that we have no lexical component in the base – for these semantic structures can be treated as the semantic interpretation of the lexical items. More important, it is easy enough to show that lexical items are very idiosyncratic in their relations (note, for instance, that I cannot say *I killed him on Thursday* if he died from wounds inflicted on Tuesday even though on Tuesday I caused him to become not alive on Thursday). It is precisely because of their idiosyncracies that lexical items are best treated in the lexicon rather than the grammar, for characteristically the lexicon is an inventory of partly unrelated items.

It is obviously beyond the scope of this book to take the discussion further. I have dealt with it at length, and at this stage of the book, because it so clearly indicates some of the basic problems of semantics. The arguments between Chomsky and his opponents are all framed in a Yes/No situation, and their arguments are thus reduced to the *Yes, it is/No, it isn't* level of argument that is typical of children's quarrels. For the arguments cannot be resolved in Yes/No terms. There is no absolute distinction between grammar and semantics, nor within semantics (or even in grammar) are there precise and uncontroversial lines of categorisation.

8.6 *Concluding remarks*

One conclusion that will be drawn from reading this book is that semantics is not a single, well-integrated discipline. It is not a clearly defined level of linguistics, not even comparable to phonology or grammar. Rather it is a set of studies of the use of language in relation to many different aspects of ex-

perience, to linguistic and non-linguistic context, to participants in discourse, to their knowledge and experience, to the
conditions under which a particular bit of language is appropriate. Indeed there is a sense in which, as we have seen,
semantics relates to the sum total of human knowledge, though
it must be the task of the linguist to limit the field of his study
and bring order to the apparent confusion and complexity.

It would be foolhardy to attempt to forecast precisely what
future trends will be. Yet there is some hope that linguists are
beginning to accept once again that semantics should not
simply be concerned with formal, semi-logical systems within
language, but is more a matter of relating language to the world
of experience. Reference (in the widest sense) is more basic
than sense. For within the wider discipline of linguistics there
has been some shift of interest away from 'pure' theory to
such topics as sociolinguistics (the study of the role of language
in society) and the acquisition of language by children.

Yet we must accept the fact that there will be no 'massive
break-through'. The complexity of semantics is merely one
aspect of the complexity of human language. What we can
say will be unprecise and often controversial. There are no
easy answers.

REFERENCES

Austin, J. L. 1962. *How to do things with words*. London: Oxford University Press.

Bach, E. & Harms, R. J. (Eds.) 1968. *Universals in linguistic theory*. New York: Holt, Rinehart and Winston.

Bazell, C. E. 1954. 'The sememe'. *Litera* 1, 17–31. In Hamp et al., pp. 329–40.

—— 1962. 'Meaning and the morpheme'. *Word* 18, 132–42.

Bazell, C. E., Catford, J. C., Halliday, M. A. K. & Robins, R. H. 1966. *In memory of J. R. Firth*. London: Longman.

Bierwisch, M. 1970. 'Semantics'. In Lyons 1970, pp. 166–84.

—— 1971. 'On classifying semantic features'. In Steinberg and Jakobovitz, pp. 410–35.

Bloomfield, L. 1933. *Language*. New York: Holt, and (1935) London: Allen and Unwin.

Bréal, M. 1900. *Semantics: studies in the science of meaning*. London: Heinemann.

Carnap, R. 1948. *Introduction to semantics*. Cambridge, Mass.: Harvard University Press.

Chomsky, N. 1959. Review of B. F. Skinner, *Verbal behaviour*. *Language* 35, 26–57. In Fodor and Katz, pp. 547–78.

—— 1957. *Syntactic structures*. The Hague: Mouton.

—— 1965. *Aspects of the theory of syntax*. Cambridge, Mass.: M.I.T. Press.

—— 1971. 'Deep structure, surface structure and semantic interpretation'. In Steinberg and Jakobovitz, pp. 183–216.

Conklin, H. C. 1935. 'Hanunóo Color'. *Southwestern Journal of Anthropology* 11, 339–44. In Hymes, pp. 189–91.

Fillmore, C. J. 1966. 'Deictic categories in the semantics of "come"'. *Foundations of Language* 2, 219–27.

—— 1968. 'The case for case'. In Bach and Harms, pp. 1–90.

Fillmore, C. J. & Langendoen, D. T. (Eds.) 1971. *Studies in linguistic semantics*. New York: Holt, Rinehart and Winston.

Firbas, J. 1959. 'Thoughts on the communicative function of the verb in English'. *Brno Studies in English* 1, 39–68.

1964. 'On defining theme in functional sentence analysis'. *Travaux linguistiques de Prague* 1, 267–80.

Firth, J. R. 1957. *Papers in Linguistics 1934–1951*. London: Oxford University Press.

Fodor, J. A. & Katz, J. J. 1956. *The structure of language: readings in the philosophy of language.* New Jersey: Prentice-Hall.

Fries, C. C. 1952. *The structure of English.* New York: Harcourt Brace, and (1957) London: Longman.

Haas, W. 1973. 'Meanings and Rules'. *Proceedings of the Aristotelian Society* 1972–3, 126–55.

Halliday, M. A. K. 1966. 'Lexis as a linguistic level'. In Bazell et al., pp. 148–62.

1967. 'Notes on transitivity and theme in English'. *Journal of Linguistics* 3, 37–81, 199–244; 4, 179–215.

Hamp, E. P., Householder, F. W. & Austerlitz, R. (Eds.) 1966. *Readings in linguistics* II. London and Chicago: Chicago University Press.

Harris, Z. S. 1951. *Methods in structural linguistics.* Chicago: Chicago University Press. Reprinted (paperback Phoenix Press) 1960 as *Structural linguistics.*

Hjelmslev, L. 1953. 'Prolegomena to a theory of language' (translated by F. J. Whitfield). *International Journal of American Linguistics* Memoir 7.

Hymes, D. (Ed.). 1964. *Language in culture and society.* New York: Harper and Row.

Joos, M. (Ed.). 1958. *Readings in linguistics.* New York: American Council of Learned Societies.

1964. *The English verb: form and meaning.* Madison: University of Wisconsin Press.

Katz, J. J. & Fodor, J. A. 1963. 'The structure of a semantic theory'. *Language* 39, 170–210. (Also in Fodor and Katz, pp. 479–518.)

Keenan, E. L. 1971. 'Two kinds of presupposition'. In Fillmore and Langendoen, pp. 45–54.

Lakoff, G. 1968. 'Instrumental adverbs and the concept of deep structure'. *Foundations of Language* 4, 4–29.

1971. 'On generative semantics'. In Steinberg and Jakobovitz, pp. 232–96.

Lyons, J. 1963. *Structural semantics.* Oxford: Blackwell.

1968. *Introduction to theoretical linguistics.* Cambridge: The University Press.

(Ed.) 1970. *New horizons in linguistics.* Harmondsworth, Middlesex: Penguin Books.

McCawley, J. D. 1968. 'The role of semantics in a grammar'. In Bach and Harms, pp. 125–70.

McIntosh, A. 1961. 'Patterns and ranges'. *Language* **37**, 325–37.

Malinowski, B. 1923. *The problem of meaning in primitive languages.* Supplement to Ogden and Richards (1923).
    1935. *Coral gardens and their magic II.* London: Allen and Unwin.

Morris, C. 1946. *Signs, language and behavior.* New York: Prentice-Hall.

Nida, E. A. 1964. *Towards a science of translating.* Leiden: Brill.

Ogden, C. K. & Richards, I. A. 1923. *The meaning of meaning.* London: Kegan Paul.

Osgood, C. E., Suci, G. J. & Tannenbaum, P. H. 1957. *The measurement of meaning.* Urbana: University of Illinois Press.

Palmer, F. R. 1974. *The English verb.* London: Longman.

Read, A. W. 1948. 'An account of the word "semantics" '. *Word* **4**, 78–97.

Russell, B. 1940. *An inquiry into meaning and truth.* London: Allen and Unwin.

Sapir, E. 1921. *Language.* New York: Harcourt Brace.
    1949. (Ed. Mandelbaum, G.). *Selected writings of Edward Sapir in language culture and personality.* Berkeley & Los Angeles: University of California Press.

de Saussure, F. 1915. *Cours de linguistique générale.* Translated (1959) as *Course in general linguistics* by Baskin, W. New York: McGraw-Hill.

Sebeok, T. A. (Ed.) 1966. *Current trends in linguistics III.* The Hague: Mouton.

Skinner, B. F. 1957. *Verbal behaviour.* New York: Appleton-Century-Crofts.

Steinberg, D. D. & Jakobovitz, L. A. (Eds.). 1971. *Semantics.* Cambridge: The University Press.

Strawson, P. F. 1964. 'Identifying reference and truth-values'. *Theoria* **30**, 96–118. In Steinberg and Jakobovitz pp. 86–99.

Ullmann, S. 1962. *Semantics: an introduction to the study of meaning.* Oxford: Basil Blackwell.

Weinreich, U. 1966. 'Explorations in semantic theory'. In Sebeok, pp. 395–477.

Whorf, B. L. 1957. (Ed. Carroll, J. B.) *Language, thought and reality: selected writings of Benjamin Lee Whorf.* Cambridge, Mass.: M.I.T. Press.

Wittgenstein, L. 1953. *Philosophical investigations.* Oxford: Blackwell.

INDEX